Index to
McMinn County,
Tennessee,

Tax Lists,
1829-1832 and 1836,
and
Detail from 1836 Tax List

Harald Reksten
and Reba Boyer

HERITAGE BOOKS
2010

HERITAGE BOOKS
AN IMPRINT OF HERITAGE BOOKS, INC.

Books, CDs, and more—Worldwide

For our listing of thousands of titles see our website at
www.HeritageBooks.com

Published 2010 by
HERITAGE BOOKS, INC.
Publishing Division
100 Railroad Ave. #104
Westminster, Maryland 21157

Copyright © 1996 Harald Reksten and Reba Boyer

All rights reserved. No part of this book may be reproduced or transmitted in any form or by any means, electronic or mechanical, including photocopying, recording or by any information storage and retrieval system without written permission from the author, except for the inclusion of brief quotations in a review.

International Standard Book Numbers
Paperbound: 978-0-7884-0490-0
Clothbound: 978-0-7884-8445-2

Table of Contents

Introduction v
Captains for 1829-1832 Tax Lists 1
Companies/Districts by Years, With Page Numbers 2
Commissioners (Tax Collectors) for 1836 Tax List 4
Location of Districts for McMinn County in 1836 5
1836 TAX LIST - DISTRICT 1 6
1836 TAX LIST - DISTRICT 2 9
1836 TAX LIST - DISTRICT 3 12
1836 TAX LIST - DISTRICT 4 15
1836 TAX LIST - DISTRICT 5 18
1836 TAX LIST - DISTRICT 6 21
1836 TAX LIST - DISTRICT 7 (ATHENS) 25
1836 TAX LIST - DISTRICT 8 29
1836 TAX LIST - DISTRICT 9 33
1836 TAX LIST - DISTRICT 10 36
1836 TAX LIST - DISTRICT 11 39
1836 TAX LIST - DISTRICT 12 43
1836 TAX LIST - DISTRICT 13 47
1836 TAX LIST - DISTRICT 14 50
1836 TAX LIST - DISTRICT 15 53
1836 TAX LIST - DISTRICT 16 (CALHOUN) 57
1836 TAX LIST - DISTRICT 17 (COLUMBUS) 61
Index to 1829-1832, 1836 McMinn Tax Lists 65

Introduction

The first version of the index to the 1829 through 1832 tax lists was compiled by Reba Boyer many years ago for her own personal use. As such it has suffered the indignities of age and some parts of it are no longer legible. Since Reba is now 90 years old I decided, with her permission, to enter her first version into the computer and reformat it to make it easier to read. At the same time I wanted to include the 1836 tax list so that a comprehensive document could be created that includes all the early (i.e. before 1840) tax lists of McMinn County. Therefore one can think of this book as a supplement to the 1830 and 1840 census records.

The original 1829-1832 tax lists are located in the McMinn County Court Clerk's Office at the Courthouse in Athens, Tennessee. The McMinn County Historical Society had the 1829-1832 tax book laminated and bound in red leather, courtesy of the Tennessee State Library and Archives in Nashville. The book is about 8" by 15" and about 1 1/2" to 2" thick.

Microfilm copies of the 1829 through 1832 tax lists are available at the Tennessee State Archives and at the Fisher Library in Athens. The original 1836 tax list is located in the Tennessee State Archives in Nashville. A printed copy exists at the Fisher Library but is now hard to read. Microfilm copies of the 1836 tax list are available at the Tennessee State Archives and at the Fisher Library in Athens.

A compilation of the 1836 Tax list was first published by the Tennessee Genealogical Society in 1989.[1] The names on that list were compared to the current transcription. Minor differences in the given name or middle initial are ignored but significant differences in

---

[1] "McMinn County Tennessee 1836 Tax List", Ansearchin News, Tennessee Genealogical Society, Vol 36 #3, pp 117-122, Vol 36 #4, pp 183-188, 1989.

surnames (i.e. differences that might prevent location in the index) are noted in the following manner. The surname interpreted for this compilation is presented first followed by a slash, "/", followed by the surname given in 1989. Both surnames are indexed. If the microfilm shows that the surname given in 1989 is wrong then the double surname is not given. The reader is encouraged to consult the original microfilm in order to resolve discrepancies.

The early tax lists, 1829 through 1832 are crudely alphabetized by militia company. The 1836 tax list is the first tax list that was organized by district. Not until the 1860 Census of McMinn County does a census record become available that breaks the county into districts to show where heads of families were residing. This book, by its inclusion of the 1836 tax list, helps to fill this void in the published records of McMinn County. It can also be used in conjunction with the 1830 and 1840 census records to show migration in and out of the county.

The 1829 Tax List spans pages 1-54, the 1830 Tax List spans pages 55-113, the 1831 Tax List spans pages 114-176, while the 1832 Tax List spans pages 177-232 of a consolidated volume of tax lists held in the Athens Courthouse. Data for the following column headings from the 1829-1832 tax lists are not included in this index: Land, White Polls, Black Polls, Town Lots, Pleasure Carriages, Stud Horses - P S. White Polls are white persons in age 21-50. The page numbers given in the index for the 1829-1832 tax payers do not refer to this book but to the original consolidated volume in Athens and the copy on microfilm. A table is given that shows all the page numbers from the original tax lists. This table can be used locate the company where each 1829-1832 taxpayer resided by taking the page number in the index and comparing to the table.

The index reference for 1836 taxpayers is different than the index reference for the 1829-1832 taxpayers. The 1836 index entry includes the number 1836 followed by a dash and then the district number of the original 1836 tax list. None of the page numbers in the index refer to this book. In order to locate the detail for a 1836 taxpayer the district given in this book must be searched. This is easy since all districts were originally alphabetized to some degree.

It should be noted that the 1836 Tax List showed taxes paid for the county and the state. The state tax was simply a portion of the total tax assessed. A small number of people were taxed a double amount. It is not known by the author why certain people were forced to pay double tax but many of the people, who had to pay double tax, were entered into the tax list after the original tax list was compiled. A "*" is used in the 1836 tax list to indicate the taxpayers that were forced to pay the double amount.

In the original tax list the surname was alphabetized according to the first letter and not always the entire surname. One district, 11, was alphabetized by given name instead of surname. This transcription follows the order of the names in the original tax list. If the original tax list placed names out of alphabetical order then the names will appear in this transcription also out of alphabetical order. If the original tax list placed the surname before the given name then this transcription does also.

The column headings for the 1836 tax list follow the original tax list. Because of the current space limitations only the most important information has been excerpted from the 1836 Tax List. This information is presented in the following columns: full name sometimes followed by a number which is the actual page number in the 1836 tax list, total acres of land owned not including school land, the value in dollars of the land, total acres of school land, the value in dollars of the school land, number of slaves between the age of 12 and 50 (along with the value in dollars of the slaves in parenthesis), number of white poles and the total tax assessed shown in dollars, cents and partial cents. If someone owned a Pleasure Carriage then this is shown in parenthesis after the person's name as PC.

In the town of Athens the number of lots and their value is substituted for the School Land. The number of lots and their value is also given in Calhoun and Columbus. All tax values have been omitted except for the total tax which included state and county tax.

At the end of each district a summary is given that shows the total number of taxpayers and slaves for each district (i.e. calculated by the author). The total district tax was copied from the original 1836 aggregate totals and also supplied. Since this can be used to contrast the wealth of the districts, it is clear that District 7 (Athens) was by far the richest district. The average value of a slave was between $450 and $500 but in Athens, which had the highest ratio of slaves to taxpayers, the value of a slave was $569. The person who paid the most taxes for one district was Charles F. Keith in District 7. He paid $29.66 1/2. It is clear by checking the detail 1836 tax list that the wealthiest people owned land in more than one district.

Harald Reksten, 1996

Captains for 1829-1832 Tax Lists

BAKER, 5-6
BARNET, 153-154, 206-207
BILLINGSLY, 22-23, 93-94, 111, 148-150
CHILDERS, 39-41, 55-56, 111, 142
CRUIZE, 47, 100-102, 112, 169, 188-189
DERICK, 82-83, 128-129, 224
DODSON, 194-195
DUGLASS, 73-74, 147, 214
EWING, 34-36, 64-66, 132-134, 204-206
FARRIS, 198-199
FIRESTONE, 17-19, 74-76, 158-160, 186-187, 221
GONCE, GOANCE, 183-185
GREENWOOD, 59-60, 146, 212-213
HILL, 1-2
JAMISON, 196-197
LEMMONS, 49-50, 98-99, 100, 112
LITTLE, 31-32
MCCULLY, 86-87, 112, 117-119, 208-209
MOONEY, 77-79, 109, 134-135
MULKEY, 67-69, 163-164, 190-191
NEWTON, 7-9
PEARSON, 119-122
PRICE, 29-30
REID, 20-21, 62-63, 144-145, 202-203
ROBERTS, 9-11, 102-104, 140-142
ROTHWELL, 24-25, 88-90, 111, 155-157
RUCKER, 14-16, 179-180
SHAMBLIN, 41-42, 108-109, 160-162, 217-218
SHARP, 122-124
SHEARMAN, 91-92, 150-152, 200-201
SHULTZ, 3-4, 84-87, 112, 137-139
SMEDLEY, 37-38, 95-97, 111, 124-125, 181-182
SMITH, 222-223
STEPHENSON, 192
SWAN, 33-34, 80-81
THOMPSON, 57-58, 130-131, 136-137, 210-211
TROTTER, 43-46, 104-107, 114-117, 226-229
TURNER, 177-178
WALKER (JAMES), 11-13, 60-62, 110-111, 126-127
WALLING, 166-168, 219-220
WHITE, 215-216
WYRICK, 26-28, 70-72

Companies/Districts by Years, With Page Numbers

1829 (Companies)

Hill 1
Shultz 3
Baker 5
Newton 7
Roberts 9
Walker 11
Rucker 14
Firestone 17
Reid 20
Billingsly 22
Rothwell 24
Wyrick 26
Price 29
Little 31
Swan 33
Ewing 34
Smedley 37
Childers 39
Shamblin 41
Trotter 43
Cruize 47
Lemmons 49

1830 (Companies)

Childers 55
Thompson 57
Greenwood 59
Walker 60
Reid 62
Ewing 64
Mulkey 67
Wyrick 70
Douglas 73
Firestone 74
Mooney 77
Swan 80
Derick 82
Shultz 84
McCully 86
Rothwell 88
Shearman 91
Billingsly 93
Smedley 95
Lemmons 98
Cruize 100
Roberts 102
Trotter 104
Shamblin 108

1831 (Companies)

Trotter 114
McCully 117
Pearson 119
Sharp 122
Smedley 124
Walker 126
Derick 128
Thompson (# 1) 130
Ewing 132
Mooney 134
Thompson (# 2) 136
Shultz 137
Roberts 140
Childers 142
Reid 144
Greenwood 146
Duglas 147
Billingsly 148
Shearman 150
Barnett 153
Rothwell 155
Firestone 158
Shamblin 160
Mulkey 163
Walling 166
Cruize 169

1832 (Companies)	1836 (Districts)
Turner 177	Dist. 1 (1-7)
Rucker 179	Dist. 2 (8-14)
Smedley 181	Dist. 3 (15-21)
Gonce 183	Dist. 4 (22-29)
Firestone (# 1) 186	Dist. 5 (30-38)
Cruize 188	Dist. 6 (39-47)
Mulkey 190	Dist. 7 (48-58)
Stephenson 192	Dist. 8 (59-69)
Dodson 194	Dist. 9 (70-76)
Jamison 196	Dist. 10 (77-84)
Farris 198	Dist. 11 (85-95)
Shearman 200	Dist. 12 (96-105)
Reid 202	Dist. 13 (106-112)
Ewing 204	Dist. 14 (113-119)
Barnett 206	Dist. 15 (120-128)
McCully 208	Dist. 16 (129-142)
Thompson 210	Dist. 17 (143-149)
Greenwood 212	
Duglas 214	
White 215	
Shamblin 217	
Walling 219	
Firestone (# 2) 221	
Smith 222	
Derick 224	
Trotter 226	

Commissioners (Tax Collectors) for 1836 Tax List

DISTRICT	COMMISSIONER	TAX PAYERS	SLAVES	TOTAL TAX
1	John Foster	102	26	$117.54 1/2[1]
2	Andrew Crawford	104	18	$88.72 1/4
3	Jesse H. Benton	97	5	$84.43
4	Elijah Hunst	114	63	$195.00
5	Benjamin Shell	117	39	$160.16 3/4
6	Abraham Bash	131	27	$174.75 3/4
7	Samuel H. Jordan (Athens)	158	106	$392.15 1/2
8	James Billingsly	162	18	$164.40
9	John Seaborn	99	20	$90.47 3/4
10	Larkin Taylor	116	29	$150.11 1/4
11	Stephen Jones	154	11	$146.40 1/2
12	J.C. Carlock	145	41	$171.08
13	Jas. Barnett	95	7	$71.94 3/4
14	Thos. Hoyle	96	36	$114.90 3/4
15	A.B. Neal	154	24	$135.93
16	John Camp (Calhoun)	154	18	$177.80
17	Henry H. Bradford (Columbus)	123	35	$156.87
TOTAL		2121[2]	521	$2592.71

---

[1] These numbers were taken directly from the summary on the microfilm.
[2] The total number of taxpayers is an approximate number based on a simple count. It should be noted that some taxpayers owned land in more than one district and therefore were listed more than once. Also some taxpayers were deceased and the tax was payed by the estate.

Location of Districts for McMinn County in 1836

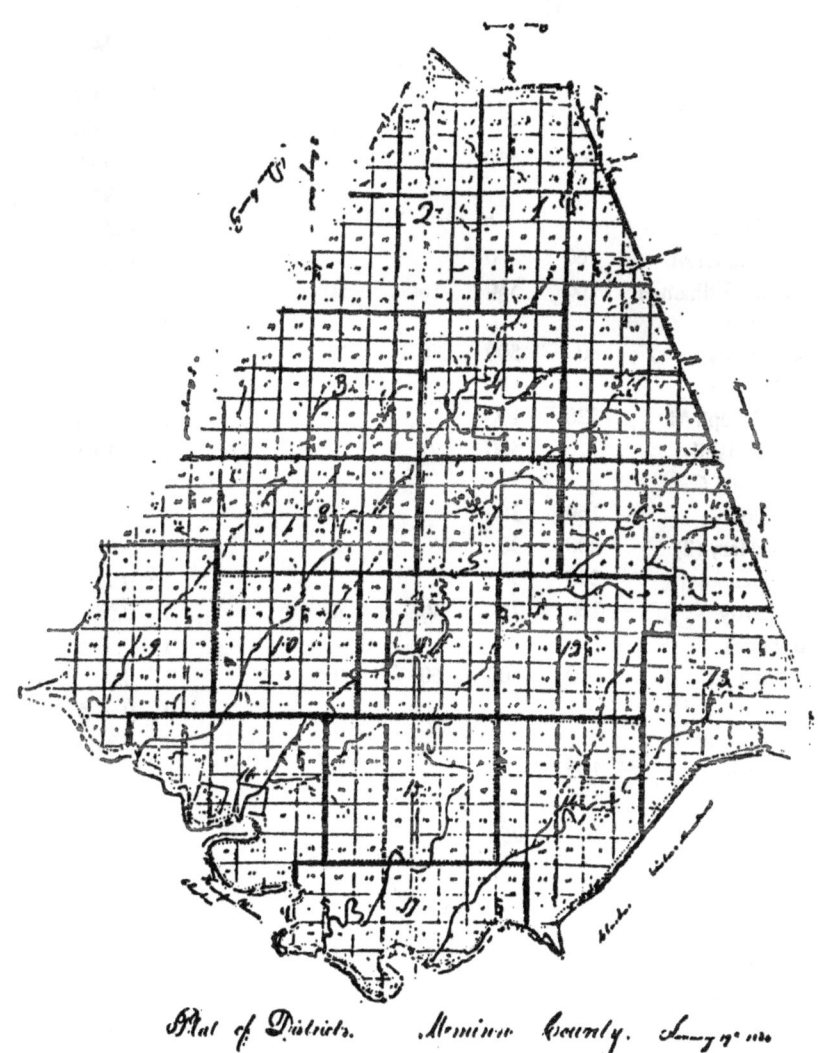

1836 TAX LIST - DISTRICT 1

NAME	ACRES	VALUE LAND	SCHOOL	VALUE	SLAVES 12 to 50	WP	TOTAL TAX
Albert, William (1)	160	500				1	1.12.5
Adams, Bird	110	50	160	50			0.07.5
Bryant, William F.	160	550	80	50			0.90.0
Bryant, Ellisan						1	0.37.5
Brown, Thomas						1	0.37.5
Blythe, Samuel M.	160	200				1	0.67.5
Breazeale, William H.	160	550	160	50		1	1.27.5
Brown, John						1	0.37.5
Brandon, Calvin	80	500	40	75			0.86.25
Birch, George							
Burnett, Joseph M.	320	1000				1	1.87.5
Burnett, Roland	110	500				1	1.12.5
Bennett, John C.						1	0.37.5
Burnett, John	160	300					0.45.0
Cannon, Mary (2)	200	300					0.45.0
Cole, James	240	500					0.75.0
Carter, Leroy	160	75	40	50		1	0.56.3
Crisp, James						1	0.37.5
Cook, John Jr.	160	500	60	100		1	0.90.0
Dean, Thomas						1	0.37.5
Day, James						1	0.37.5
Davis, Lewis	160	100					0.15.0
Dotson, William	177	350					0.52.5
Davis, Aaron	60	250					0.37.5
Davis, John						1	0.37.5
Dotson, Doctor F.						1	0.37.5
Ellis, William						1	0.37.5
Fry, Newell C.	80	300				1	0.82.5
Fitch, Isaac (3)	160	400				1	0.97.5
Fitch, Jacob						1	0.37.5
Fry, John						1	0.37.5
Field, Thomas			80	100		1	0.52.5
Forster, William	135	800			1 (500)	1	2.32.5
Fitzgarrel, Joseph	565	3800	200	200	1 (700)	1	7.42.5

Name							
Fry, Austin	80	500	110	75		1	1.23.75
Fortner, William						1	0.37.5
Fry, Philip	167	1200	120	200			2.10.25
Forster, Thomas						1	0.37.5
Forster, John & Chrisley	480	2200	120	750		1	3.78.75
Foster, Andrew						1	0.37.5
Garrison, Robert	200	600					0.90.0
Glase, Henry	400	3000				1	4.87.5
Grisham, Thomas						1	0.37.5
Glase, John (4)						1	0.37.5
Golden, Jacob	304	800	320	260			1.50.0
Golden, William						1	0.37.5
Hicks, Stephen						1	0.37.5
Hawks, William			240	275		1	0.78.75
Howell, James	80	300				1	0.82.5
Hancock, Martin						1	0.37.5
Harrelston, William	160	280					0.37.5
Harden, Joseph	175	800				1	1.57.5
Hughbank, George						1	0.37.5
Jamerson, David F.	160	1200	40	5		1	2.18.25
Kirkpartrick, John	520	1978	320	22			2.99.5
Lasey, Levi						1	0.37.5
Lacas, Robert	160	400					0.60.0
McClary, James						1	0.37.5
Maise, James (*)	160	180					0.24.0
Moody, John (5)	280	800				1	1.57.5
Manis, Ephraim						1	0.37.5
McCully, Alexander						1	0.37.5
Moors, Caleb	80	150			2 (1100)	1	2.25.0
McCall, Sarah	160	400	80	50			0.67.5
Neil, John	240	1400	40	100			2.25.0
Owen, George P.						1	0.37.5
Lovey, Pearson	320	1000					1.50.0
Prigmore, Thomas	1180	5700	384	384	14(6650)	1	19.47.5
Redding, Rebecca	160	150					0.22.5
Redding, Thomas						1	0.37.5
Rutherford, William						1	0.37.5
Rutherford, James	230	700					1.05.0
Roberd, James	160	1100					1.50.0
Roberd, William						1	0.37.5

Name							
Richardson, James (6)			160	160			0.24.0
Richardson, Jesse			80	80			0.12.0
Small, John	160	800				1	1.57.5
Small, Henry						1	0.37.5
Stone, Ambrose	144	400				1	0.97.5
Sligar, Adam	391	750	80	100	1 (500)	1	2.40.0
Shipley, Elizabeth	160	500			1 (400)		1.35.0
Shipley, James						1	0.37.5
Smith, Joseph						1	0.37.5
Stone, John	320	1200					1.80.0
StandsBury, Isreal						1	0.37.5
StandsBury, Samuel						1	0.37.5
Shipley, Randolph R.						1	0.37.5
Shoemaker, John						1	0.37.5
Taylor, John						1	0.37.5
Thomas, James	280	1200			5 (3100)		6.45.0
Thim, Anderson (7)	312	1560	160	160		1	2.95.5
Thomas, James Jr.					1 (500)	1	1.12.5
Thomas, Jonathan	100	300					0.45.0
Vestall, James	300	500				1	1.12.5
Winkle, Abraham	80	300				1	0.83.5
Wallen, Thomas	160	500	120	50			0.82.5
Wallace, George	214	400				1	0.97.5
Weaver, Adam						1	0.37.5
Wasson, Jonas	240	615	160	150		1	1.52.5
Whitehead, Frances			160	125			0.18.25
Wallin, John						1	0.37.5

Total Taxpayers: 102, Slaves: 26, Taxes Collected: $117.54.5

1836 TAX LIST - DISTRICT 2

NAME	ACRES	VALUE	SCHOOL LAND	VALUE	SLAVES 12 to 50	WP	TOTAL TAX
Butrame, Noah (8)	300	800	80	200		1	1.87.5
Branham, Jefferson	20	100	40	50		1	0.60.0
Butram, Jacob	160	500					0.75.0
Burnes, William	158	100					0.90.0
Bower, John	160	300				1	0.82.5
Beck, John H.			160	100			0.15.0
Brittian, Nathaniel	160	300				1	0.82.5
Bottam/Bottom, Allen	120	400					0.60.0
Boggas, Abijah	320	200					0.50.0
Batrum/Butram, Hial	230	700				1	1.42.5
Batram/Butram, James						1	0.37.5
Carroll, Luke	160	570					0.75.0
Carroll, Henry	240	600				1	1.27.5
Clark, Jesse						1	0.37.5
Crisman, Isaac			170	125			0.18.25
Carrington, James (9)						1	0.37.5
Cloud, James						1	0.37.5
Crew, Katherine	100	200					0.30.0
Coppack, Aaron						1	0.37.5
Christian, James						1	0.37.5
Churchmell, George W.			60	60			0.09.0
Cloud, George W.	120	200				1	0.67.3
Crow, Wilson			180	300		1	0.82.5
Crawford, Andrew	170	400	184	300			0.60.0
Dyer, James	159.5	300	80	75		1	0.93.75
Dyer, Thomas H.	160	300					0.45.0
Dodson, John						1	0.37.5
Darter, John	1120	1700					2.55.0
Dodson, William	320	1400			3 (1100)		3.75.0
Dodson, Allen						1	0.37.5
Dyer, William (10)						1	0.37.5
Ellison, Hinson	240	400	40	10			0.61.5
Fields, Green	45	125				1	0.56.25
Fields, John & Thomas	160	900	60	100		1	1.87.5

Fields, Beeson	450	600	100	150		1	1.50.0
Gaunce, Abraham			80	25			0.0.75
Gallant, James	540	1400					2.10.0
Gallant, William						1	0.37.5
Gaddy, Richard						1	0.37.5
Golden, Abraham	59	100	80	50			0.22.25
Hicks, James	160	160					0.24.0
Hackler, John			120	300		1	0.82.5
Harmon, Leonard						1	0.37.5
Hickman, Samuel L.			80	50			0.07.5
Harmon, Jacob						1	0.37.5
Hackler, Robert (11)						1	0.37.5
Haney, Stephen						1	0.37.5
Haney, John						1	0.37.5
Hardin, Joseph			40	40			0.06.0
Hackler, George	160	250	60	100			0.52.5
Ivey, Hartwell	320	1200	160	160		1	2.41.5
Ivey, Ausley			60	60		1	0.46.5
Jones, William	173.5	450					0.67.5
Johnson, Henry						1	0.37.5
King, John	100	350				1	0.90.0
Kennedy, James	80	400	40	100			0.75.0
Kennedy, Thomas R.						1	0.37.5
Kitchen, John	110	300	80	100			0.60.0
Latham, Henry	380	800			2 (1000)	1	3.07.5
Lacy, William	130	400					0.60.0
Lewelling, Lewis (12)						1	0.37.5
Love, Edward			40	50			0.07.5
Monroe, Robert						1	0.37.5
McCoy, Daniel			80	20			0.03.0
McCall, Sarah	320	350					0.52.5
Mendenhall, John	360	360					0.54.0
Marsh, Alfred	480	600				1	1.27.5
Miller, William L.	80	150				1	0.60.0
Monroe, George	720	1980	80	20			3.00.0
Matlock, Charles	480	1000					1.50.0
Menton/Minton,Johnson	120	320	100	30		1	0.90.0
McPhail, Neil	320	1200	120	30		1	2.22.0
McPhail, Dugald						1	0.37.5
McPhail, John						1	0.37.5

McPhail, Daniel	160	600					1	1.27.5
Newman, Bird (13)	160	800				1 (500)	1	2.32.5
Newman, Jesse							1	0.37.5
Newman, Bird Jr.							1	0.37.5
Neely, William H.	165	800					1	1.57.5
Purcell, Daniel	360	800				9 (4500)		7.95.0
Pearson, William L.	200	275	40	25		1 (400)	1	1.42.5
Riddle, Samuel L.	160	400	80	80				0.72.0
Riddle, James							1	0.37.5
Riddle, John							1	0.37.5
Rogers, John	100	700					1	1.42.5
Scott, Jesse	80	200					1	0.67.5
Spencer, James	130	500					1	1.12.5
Slager, Henry	160	400	80	100			1	1.12.5
Sharpe, David							1	0.37.5
Spencer, Levy	80	450	40	40				0.73.5
Smith, John (14)							1	0.37.5
Sligar, Thomas	320	1200				2 (700)	1	3.22.5
Sallee, Masey	160	100						0.15.0
Sellers, Mertle	160	450						0.67.5
Smith, Theophilas			40	5				0.0.75
Shoemaker, John			40	80				0.12.0
Wan, Robert	190	450					1	1.05.0
White, Barton			251.5	300			1	0.82.5
Wassom, Coonrod			80	150				0.22.5
West, Enoch							1	0.37.5
West, Jesse							1	0.37.5
Wright, William	125	30					1	0.42.0
Willen/Witten, James	240	750						1.12.5

Total Taxpayers: 104, Slaves: 18, Taxes Collected: $88.72.25

1836 TAX LIST - DISTRICT 3

NAME	ACRES	VALUE LAND	SCHOOL	VALUE	SLAVES 12 to 50	WP	TOTAL TAX
Allen, Cox & West (15)	86	175				1	0.63.75
Atkinson, Jonas						1	0.37.5
Butranam, Allen	405	600				1	1.27.5
Benton, Jesse H.	222	440					0.66.0
Bogguss, Abijah			80	80			0.12.0
Bodine, James	200	250					0.37.5
Beaver, James						1	0.37.5
Bishop, Joseph						1	0.37.5
Bishop, Isaac						1	0.37.5
Bishop, James			160	25			0.03.75
Baker, Alexander	190	600					0.90.0
Casey, John						1	0.37.5
Coates, William						1	0.37.5
Coffey, James	65	100				1	0.52.5
Culton, James	403	1600					2.40.0
Culton, Hugh M. (16)						1	0.37.5
Casey, Ambler	320	1000					1.50.0
Casey, Moses						1	0.37.5
Cliuge/Cleage, Samuel	320	1000					1.50.0
Cook, Judiah						1	0.37.5
Coates, John						1	0.37.5
Cruise, Gilbert	175	2000				1	3.37.5
Dennis, Isom	150	150				1	0.60.0
Dennis, James	110	360	40	40		1	0.97.5
Dickerson, Thomas I.	80	150				1	0.60.0
Davis, Elie	120	120					0.18.0
Gollys, James	298	510					0.75.0
Grisham, John	75	500				1	1.12.5
Grisham, Michael						1	0.37.5
Guthrey, Thomas						1	0.37.5
Green, William H. (17)			320	200			0.30.0
Hodge, Anderson	450	1350				1	2.40.0
Hart, John P.						1	0.37.5
Hampton, Zachariah			100	100			0.15.0

Name							
Hart, John Sr.	160	500					0.75.0
Hudson, Robert B.	360	650				1	1.35.0
Hays, James	160	300					0.45.0
Harvie/Havid, Ridden						1	0.37.5
Isom, John	160	400				1	0.97.5
Isom, William						1	0.37.5
Isom, Bolin						1	0.37.5
Isom, Charles	155	400					0.60.0
Jordan, Robt. W.						1	0.37.5
Jones, William Jr.	160	160				1	0.61.5
Knox, William	305	450				1	1.05.0
Knox, James (18)	157	400				1	0.97.5
Keten, Benton	360	900	160	100		1	1.87.5
Lawson, Allen	80	400				1	0.97.5
Lawson, Jacob Sr.			240	500			0.75.0
Lawson, Jacob Jr.	160	150				1	0.60.0
Lawson, Andrew	160	350				1	0.70.0
Lawson, Nathan Sr.	160	500					0.75.0
Lawson, Richard	120	200				1	0.47.0
Lawson, Nathan Jr.						1	0.37.5
Lawson, Tiny	321	500				1	1.12.5
Lawson, Hugh	200	350				1	0.90.0
Lawson, David Jr.	360	1000				1	1.87.5
Lawson, David Sr.	420	600					0.90.0
Lawson, James	160	400					0.60.0
Moore, Samuel	120	330					0.49.5
Moore, Thomas	160	200				1	0.67.5
Moore, Alexander (19)						1	0.37.5
Matlock, Charles	200	400	80	50			0.67.5
Morris, William N.	300	1000			3 (1200)	1	3.67.5
Mcmahan, John	160	1200				1	2.17.5
Mitcalf, Charles	400	400					0.60.0
McChristen, Robert						1	0.37.5
Miller, Elijah L.						1	0.37.5
Owens, John						1	0.37.5
Power, Holloway	680	2500					3.75.0
Plank, Benedict						1	0.37.5
Plank, Christen	160	300					0.45.0
Plank, Hiram						1	0.37.5
Rogers, Lawson	150	300				1	0.82.5

Rouden, Asa	320	600	100	100		1	1.42.5
Rouden, James						1	0.37.5
Rouden, John (20)			240	300		1	0.82.5
Royster, Charles H.	320	500				1	1.12.5
Roberts, Benjamin	155	400					0.60.0
Rothwell, Richard	17	100				1	0.52.5
Stockton, Daniel D.	440	625				1	1.31.25
Snider, Robert	80	150				1	0.60.0
Stewart, William	275	800				1	1.57.5
Spradlin, Richard Sr.	420	1200					1.80.0
Spradlin, Richard Jr.						1	0.37.5
Smith, Joel			160	100		1	0.52.5
Smith, Edward						1	0.37.5
Shelton, Stinson B.			280	500		1	1.37.5
Thomas, Jonathan	920	2000				1	3.37.5
Tally, Willis			210	210		1	0.67.5
Wheeler, Samuel						1	0.37.5
Wheeler, James (PC)	160	400				1	0.97.5
Waumuck, John (21)	160	280	40	20	1 (200)	1	1.12.5
Wilson, John						1	0.37.5
Wade, James	167	400				1	0.97.5
WaltenBarger, Michael	250	620				1	1.30.5
WaltenBarger, Peter	320	600			1 (300)	1	1.72.5

Total Taxpayers: 97, Slaves: 5, Taxes Collected: $84.43

1836 TAX LIST - DISTRICT 4

NAME	ACRES	VALUE LAND	SCHOOL	VALUE	SLAVES 12 to 50	WP	TOTAL TAX
Arnwine, John (22)	450	3000			2 (800)		5.70.0
Arnwine, Albertes	310	1600			1 (400)	1	3.37.5
Albert, James						1	0.37.5
Anderson, William						1	0.37.5
Adams, Burgess						1	0.37.5
Anderson, Isaac	160	1500			1 (400)	1	3.22.5
Adkins, Leomon						1	0.37.5
Belcher, John						1	0.37.5
Burch, Henry	81	350				1	0.90.0
Braxly/Bradly, Widow	80	100					0.15.0
Bealer, Joseph						1	0.37.5
Brown, A.B.	145	200					0.30.0
Burns, William	85	1500				1	2.62.5
Butram, Larkin	320	1500				1	2.62.5
Ballew, William	160	700					1.05.0
Calloway, William S.					2 (1100)	1	2.02.5
Crismon, Nealy (23)	163	775	80	25		1	1.57.5
Christian, John	80	250				1	0.75.0
Crawford, John						1	0.37.5
Collins, George						1	0.37.5
Cate, Thomas	376	2380			4 (1800)		6.27.0
Cate, Elijah	376	2500			3 (1400)	1	6.22.5
Cate, William	153	850				1	1.65.0
Centers, F.K.	220	900	160	100	1 (500)	1	2.62.5
Cliage/Cleage, Samuel	966	4550			8 (4900)		14.17.5
Cain, W.D.						1	0.37.5
Derrick, Jonathan						1	0.37.5
Davis, Brittian						1	0.37.5
Dodd, John	160	600			1 (400)		1.50.0
Ellison, Hinson	120	600			1 (500)	1	2.02.5
Ellison, Benjamin (24)						1	0.37.5
Elledge, Jacob						1	0.37.5
Faulkner, R.	160	400			1 (500)	1	1.72.5
Franklin, D.						1	0.37.5

Name							
Gass, John	220	5000					4.50.0
Foster, Benjamin						1	0.37.5
Gass, Allen						1	0.37.5
Gass, John						1	0.37.5
Goodwin, James	153	200				1	0.67.5
Gruble, William						1	0.37.5
Grisham, Simeon						1	0.37.5
Goleham, Isaac						1	0.37.5
Gord, Miles						1	0.37.5
Hardin, M.						1	0.37.5
Hill, William						1	0.37.5
Hill, Claborn (25)	86	860				1	1.66.5
Hill, Joabb	554	3150			1 (500)		5.47.5
Hurst, Elijah	392	2000			3 (1500)		5.25.0
Hurst, Russel	293	1600				1	2.77.5
Hurst, John L.	240	1000				1	1.87.5
Hicks, James	310	700					1.05.0
Humphreys, Jn.						1	0.37.5
Haile, Franklin						1	0.37.5
Isaacs, C.W.						1	0.37.5
John, Ezekiel	66	200				1	0.67.5
John, Thomas	155	600				1	1.27.5
Johnson, Madison						1	0.37.5
Johnson, Saml.						1	0.37.5
Keith, C.F.	480	4800	160	350			7.65.0
Keith, Partrick P.						1	0.37.5
Keeton, Littleton						1	0.37.5
Keeton, William						1	0.37.5
Lyle, Martha	30	60					0.09.0
Lane, John	160	600					0.90.0
Lane, Isaac	160	130					0.19.5
Lawson, Lacy						1	0.37.5
Morrison, Joseph B.						1	0.37.5
Minze, Joseph	180	1000			1 (400)	1	2.47.5
Matlock, Charles					1 (700)	1	1.42.5
Matlock, Henry	700	4000			7 (3200)	1	11.17.5
Morrison, Nat.						1	0.37.5
McRictor/McRector, M.	80	80	160	20			0.15.0
McPherson, Widow	100	250					0.37.5
McPherson, Ann			80	20			0.03.0

Name					
Miller, John	160	1600	1 (500)	1	3.15.0
Miller, Leven (27)				1	0.37.5
Mitcalf, Charles (PC)	800	5000	6 (2800)	1	12.52.5
Mathews, Aaron Estate	140	800			1.20.0
Moore, John	380	2000	1 (500)		3.75.0
Moore, John				1	0.37.5
Moore, William				1	0.37.5
Martin, Samuel	160	100			0.15.0
Neill, John	240	1500	4 (1900)		5.10.0
Neill, Anderson				1	0.37.5
Orr, Mary	197	2500	1 (200)		3.75.0
Orr, Joseph L.				1	0.37.5
Orr, John W.				1	0.37.5
Pursell, Widow	100	280			0.37.5
Patt, John G.					0.37.5
Rider, John				1	0.37.5
Robbins, Hance (28)				1	0.37.5
Ripley, Jacob				1	0.37.5
Robinson, Elizabeth	80	100			0.15.0
Rutherford, Nehimiah				1	0.37.5
Shadle, James				1	0.37.5
Suthard, Gillum	160	400		1	0.97.5
Small, James	170	500		1	1.12.52
Shell, James				1	0.37.5
Saller/Sallee, John				1	0.37.5
Sellers, Edmond				1	0.37.5
Smith, Nat.	1160	7000	6 (3150)	1	15.60.0
Smith, Stephen	200	1200			1.80.0
Smith, Isaiah	160	700		1	1.42.5
Smith, D. Estate	560	1200	1 (500)		2.55.0
Tipton, Esau				1	0.37.5
Wassom, Lonas (29)	80	100			0.15.0
Witt, James	185	600		1	1.27.5
Weathen/Weathers, Joseph				1	0.37.5
Webb, Joseph				1	0.37.5
Webb, Martin				1	0.37.5
Wilson, James	720	3400	4 (1800)		7.80.0
Wilson, Wm.			1 (400)	1	0.97.5
Wilson, Joseph				1	0.37.5

West, William		1	0.37.5
Wryht, Robert		1	0.37.5

Total Taxpayers: 114, Slaves: 63, Taxes Collected: $195.00

1836 TAX LIST - DISTRICT 5

NAME	ACRES	VALUE LAND	SCHOOL	VALUE	SLAVES 12 to 50	WP	TOTAL TAX
Anderson, Martin (30)						1	0.37.5
Ballew, William	160	2000			6 (3000)		7.50.0
(same)	160	500					
(same)	90	1000					
(same)	160	500					3.00.0
Ballew, Jefferson						1	0.37.5
Ballew, William H.						1	0.37.5
Burn, Adam	47	300				1	0.82.5
Beegles, David						1	0.37.5
Boyd, John						1	0.37.5
Blase/Blare, Samuel	32	120					0.18.0
Boyd, Herbid	200	800				1	1.57.5
Balys, Pike						1	0.37.5
Brown, Joseph						1	0.37.5
Beavers, Berry						1	0.37.5
Cunningham, Wm. H.	453	1695	360	54			2.73.5
Christen, Lewis (31)	320	1100				1	2.02.5
Cunningham, Wm.H. Jr.						1	0.37.5
Christen, Jesse						1	0.37.5
Carter, Charles	160	700			3 (1600)		3.45.0
Colier, Wilson						1	0.37.5
Cunningham, John	190	800				1	1.57.5
Dobs, Hezekiah						1	0.37.5
Dobs, Hiram						1	0.37.5
Emerson, Allen						1	0.37.5
Forrest, James						1	0.37.5
Fair, Thomas						1	0.37.5
Gibson, George	190	2140	80	60			3.30.0

Name							
Goddard, Thornton	480	2200				1	3.67.5
Goddard, Hugh						1	0.37.5
Gibson, Robert (32)						1	0.37.5
Garret, Washington						1	0.37.5
Garret, Calvin						1	0.37.5
Hill, Joabb	80	350					0.52.5
Hill, Isaac						1	0.37.5
Hill, Thomas						1	0.37.5
Hix, John						1	0.37.5
Hill, William	168	1000				1	1.87.5
Henderson, C.S.	130	700				1	1.42.5
Holt, Sarrah	223.3	1500					2.25.0
Holt, Jane	93.3	500					0.75.0
Holt, Serena	140	500					0.75.0
Holt, Thomas	90	500					0.75.0
Holt, Frances A.	93.3	500					0.75.0
Hartly, John	160	400	160	100			0.75.0
Hail, Samuel (33)	79	650				1	1.35.0
Hightower, Wm.						1	0.37.5
Hartley, Lorenzo	160	200				1	0.67.5
Haney, William S.	140	700					1.05.0
Isbell, Benjamin (PC)	319	2400			3 (1400)		6.00.0
John, Thomas	160	400					0.60.0
John, Robert	320	300				1	0.82.5
John, William	240	350					0.52.5
John, Andrew	160	50					0.07.25
Key, William						1	0.37.5
Key, Thomas						1	0.37.5
King, Alfred	175	800				1	1.57.5
Lane, Russel	160	860	40	40	1 (400)	1	2.32.5
Lane, Tidence	110	700			1 (300)	1	1.87.5
Lowry, James Sr.	478	2700			3 (1100)		5.70.0
Lowry, Isaac (34)	240	1200	80	80		1	2.29.5
Lowry, Daniel	400	1600	160	200	1 (600)	1	3.97.5
Lowry, James Jr.						1	0.37.5
Lowry, John						1	0.37.5
Lane, Isaac	107	1070			1 (500)		2.35.0
Lane, John	9	200				1	0.67.5
Lee, Samuel						1	0.37.5
Lusk, John	155	800	80	10	1 (400)		1.81.5

Name							
Lusk, Hugh						1	0.37.5
Maxwell, Robert	160	800					1.20.0
Morris, Dickerson	320	700					1.05.0
McGee, John	640	6400					9.60.0
Mathews, John	146	2000				1	3.37.5
Mathews, James						1	0.37.5
Mashborn, John						1	0.37.5
Mendenall, Isaac (35)						1	0.37.5
McKeehan, Jobe	320	1000				1	1.87.5
McKeehan, Aaron	160	700				1	1.42.5
McKeehan, James						1	0.37.5
McDanall, Wm.	160	500				1	1.37.5
McBee, Alexander	160	400				1	0.97.5
McCroy, Charles	160	1200				1	2.17.5
Netherland, James W.	160	1500			4 (2500)	1	6.37.5
Peter, Isaac						1	0.37.5
Pickens, Nancy	126	300					0.45.0
Samuel Pugh						1	0.37.5
Patterson, Robt.						1	0.37.5
Reagan, Jas. H.	593.3	4000			8 (3000)		10.87.5
Rice, Martha	210	2000			4 (2000)		6.00.0
Rice, Henry	78	600					0.90.0
Roberson, John (36)						1	0.37.5
Rusten, John						1	0.37.5
Smith, Sharkman D.						1	0.37.5
Smith, Joseph	260	1000				1	1.87.5
Smith, Henderson	50	500				1	1.12.5
Small, William	117	900					1.35.0
Small, James						1	0.37.5
Small, William W.						1	0.37.5
Small, Wilson						1	0.37.5
Stead, Henry	160	800					1.20.0
Steed, Thomas	105	50				1	0.45.0
Sherman, Thomas	250	1000	200	105			1.65.75
Sherman, John						1	0.37.5
Stalkup, Moses	136	600				1	1.27.5
Stow, Solomon						1	0.37.5
Stow, Robert (37)						1	0.37.5
Stow, Samuel						1	0.37.5
Trout, John	160	1000	80	100			1.50.0

Name	Acres	Value			Slaves		Tax
Thomas, Williamson	354	1200					1.80.0
Terry, William	480	2000			3 (1200)		4.80.0
Trout, Mathew						1	0.37.5
Trout, William						1	0.37.5
Thomas, William Jr.						1	0.37.5
Thomas, Jonathan						1	0.37.5
Thos., James						1	0.37.5
Weri/Ware, George	73						----
Wilson, Samuel	160	400					0.60.0
Wilson, David	101	800					1.20.0
Wright, Sydney	215	200				1	0.67.5
Winton, George			120	120			0.18.0

Total Taxpayers: 117, Slaves: 39, Taxes Collected: $160.16.75

1836 TAX LIST - DISTRICT 6

NAME	ACRES	VALUE LAND	SCHOOL	VALUE	SLAVES 12 to 50	WP	TOTAL TAX
Airhart, Peter (39)	70	600				1	1.27.5
Allen, John	154	700					1.05.0
Allen, Benjamin						1	0.37.5
Adams, John						1	0.37.5
Browder, Joseph	460	2200			3 (1400)	2	6.15.0
Bond, Joshua	110	500				1	1.12.5
Blair, J.L.	30.5	400				1	0.97.5
Bond, Benjamin	237	1200			2 (800)	1	3.37.5
Barnet, John W.	300	1200				1	2.17.5
Boon, Israel	145	600					0.90.0
Barnet, William	160	700					1.05.0
Barnet, James M.	180	600				1	1.27.5
Barb, Abraham	280	2000				1	3.37.5
Bond, Simon	235	1200				1	2.17.5
Bond, Joana	205	1500					2.25.0
Baker, John (40)	160	300				1	0.82.5
Bond, Benjamin	139	600			2 (1000)	1	2.77.5
Bryant, Elisha	161	1300				1	2.32.5
Brown, Benjamin	160	200					0.30.0
Bryant, Katherine	160	400					0.60.0

Name					
Barger, George	200	300		1	0.62.5
Blackborn/Blackhorn, James				1	0.37.5
Bryant, John W.P.				1	0.37.5
Cricket, James	110	350		1	0.90.0
Coffey, Marvel	150	700		1	1.42.5
Cooper, Thomas	90	550		1	1.20.0
Cooper, James	70	400		1	0.97.5
Canseler, John	155	1000		1	1.87.5
Cooper, Bennet	200	1000		1	1.87.5
Cooper, Philip	160	800	2 (1000)		2.70.0
Carter, Charles (41)	140	200			0.30.0
Cunningham, Moses	370	1800		1	3.07.5
Chapman, Lemuel	320	1200		1	2.17.5
Cunningham, Evaline	160	400			0.60.0
Carter, Arasmus				1	0.37.5
Cartrite, John				1	0.37.5
Carter, Edmund				1	0.37.5
Crocket, David				1	0.37.5
Dilday, Elias	73	75		1	0.48.75
Dixon, Elie	151	800		1	1.57.5
Dixon, Samuel W.	80	500		1	1.12.5
Dodson, William	530	1600		1	2.77.5
Dodson, Fanny	230	800			1.20.0
Elliott, Jesse	400	770			1.15.5
Elliott, J.M.			1 (450)	1	1.05.0
Ellis, Joshua (42)	200	800			1.20.0
Fain, Ebenezer	160	1100	2 (800)		2.85.0
Felker, Peter	160	600		1	1.27.5
Frazure, Thomas				1	0.37.5
Gregory, Robert	305	1500		1	2.62.5
Garet/Gant, James	120	600		1	1.27.5
Hamilton, Joseph	320	1800	2 (1000)	1	4.57.5
Harroll, John	301	800		1	1.57.5
Haney, William S.	360	600			0.90.0
Hail, Lewis	186	400	1 (400)	1	1.57.5
Hix, Martin M.	804	1300		1	0.82.5
Hardy, Samuel	304	1200	1 (400)	1	2.77.5
Hix, Shadrick	132	400			0.60.0
Hill, John	160	400			0.60.0

Hall, Nathaniel				1	0.37.5
Hix, Isaac (43)				1	0.37.5
Hammons, Elisha				1	0.37.5
Hardy, James				1	0.37.5
Harril, Enoch				1	0.37.5
Hawkins, Joseph	96	400			0.60.0
Julian, Isom	137	1300		1	2.32.5
Julian, George	118	300		1	0.82.5
Killingsworth, Joseph				1	0.37.5
Lasiter, Wiley	320	1700			2.55.0
Lee, William	330	3500	3 (1500)		7.50.0
Low, Isaac	160	550			0.82.5
Lasiter, Jonathan				1	0.37.5
Low, James				1	0.37.5
Love, John M.				1	0.37.5
Lewis, Edmund				1	0.37.5
Moore, Jesse C. (44) (*)	324	1800		1	6.15.0
McRoberts, Samuel	90	400		1	0.97.5
McRoberts, Andrew	70	400		1	0.97.5
Martin, John	317	1200			1.80.0
Miller, John	160	400			0.60.0
Middleton, John	160	1200			1.50.0
McGuire, Henry	120	500			0.75.0
Miller, John				1	0.37.5
McKeehan, George H.				1	0.37.5
Miller, Morgan				1	0.37.5
Middleton, Hugh				1	0.37.5
North, George				1	0.37.5
Orr, James				1	0.37.5
Officer, Samuel W.				1	0.37.5
Odonall, Thomas				1	0.37.5
Patty, Obadiah (45)	516	2600			3.90.0
Patty, George O.	254	800		1	1.57.5
Porter, Andrew	202	500		1	1.12.5
Patty, Benjamin	350	1500		1	2.62.5
Philips, Charles	194	800			1.20.0
Philips, ElKany				1	0.37.5
Pangle, Andrew				1	0.37.5
Pyram, James F.				1	0.37.5
Pack, Jeremiah				1	0.37.5

Name							
Robison, Thomas	160	400			1 (400)		1.20.0
Robeson, Daniel	160	400				1	0.97.52
Reynolds, George	320	1500				1	2.62.5
Rice, Limon	160	600					0.90.0
Robison, Joseph			160	50			0.07.5
Richey, John						1	0.37.5
Swan, Robert M. (46)	160	1200			1 (400)	1	2.77.5
St. John, Nathan	110	260				1	0.76.5
Stephenson, Edward	80	550				1	1.20.0
Swan, John						1	0.37.5
Smith, John	240	2000				1	3.37.5
Smith, Israel	230	2000				1	3.37.5
Smith, Joseph	230	2450				1	4.05.0
Smith, Mary	160	400					0.60.0
Smith, Robert	110	500				1	1.12.5
Smith, David	50	300				1	0.82.5
Smith, John	190	300				1	0.82.5
Smith, William						1	0.37.5
Smith, William Sr.						1	0.37.5
Smith, William						1	0.57.5
Torbett, John	50	800	160	50		1	0.90.0
Thornton, Charles T.(47)					2 (800)	1	1.57.5
Tuck, Joseph						1	0.37.5
Tuck, William						1	0.37.5
Wiggings, William	447	2900			2 (1000)		5.85.0
Walker, Elias	171	600				1	1.27.5
Wilson, Samuel	160	600			2 (900)	1	2.62.5
Wiggings, John						1	0.37.5
Watson, William						1	0.37.5
Watson, George						1	0.37.5
Watson, James						1	0.37.5
Watson, John						1	0.37.5

Total Taxpayers: 131, Slaves: 27, Taxes Collected: $174.75.75

1836 TAX LIST - DISTRICT 7 (ATHENS)

NAME	ACRES	VALUE	SCHOOL LAND	VALUE	SLAVES 12 to 50	WP	TOTAL TAX
William W. Anderson	20	200	5 lots	3500	1 (400)	1	6.52.5
Thomas Akin (48)						1	0.37.5
Francis Boyd						1	0.37.5
Solomon Bogart	20	700	3.5 lots	2900		1	5.77.5
John L. Bridges	57	150	1 lot	500		1	1.12.5
James S. Bridges			1 lot	50	2 (900)	1	2.02.5
John W.M. Breazial			2 lots	1300		1	2.32.5
Julius W. Blackwell					2 (1500)	1	2.62.5
Spenser Beaver	72.5	800			1 (500)	1	2.32.5
J.W. Browder			1 lot	450		1	0.45.0
William Ballew			1 lot	400		1	0.60.0
James F. Bradford			1 lot	600			1.27.5
William O. Barnett					1 (450)		0.67.5
James W. Barrett						1	0.37.5
Joel K. Brown	5	35	3 lots	2805	1 (400)	1	4.23.5
James Baker						1	0.37.5
Edmund Browder (49)	340.5	1200			1 (400)	1	2.40.0
Mathew Browder						1	0.37.5
Patton A. Bradford					3 (1400)	1	2.47.5
George Bush						1	0.37.5
A.B. Brown (*)			1 lot	300		1	1.65.0
Charles Bogart	160	800				1	1.57.5
Isaac Crow	3	75	1 lot	1000		1	1.98.75
William H. Cook			1 lot	200			0.30.0
Reubon Casada	485	4000					6.00.0
John C. Casada						1	0.37.5
David Casada						1	0.37.5
Alexander Cleage			0.5 lot	350	2 (850)	1	2.17.5
William Cunningham			1 lot	600			0.90.0
John Crawford			3.5 lots	3250	2 (1200)	1	7.05.0
Marshall W. Cunningham	200	400				1	0.97.5
Randolph Carter (50)			1 lot	2000		1	3.37.5
Simeon Cate	240	1000	1 lot	50	1 (400)	1	1.87.5
David Cliago/Cleage			1 lot	50	1 (400)	1	1.05.0

Name							
William Clark (PC)	80	125				1	0.86.5
Victor M. Campbell			2 lots	800		1	1.57.5
Ebenezer Cooper			1 lot	200		1	0.67.5
Thomas Crutchfield	260	720	7 lots	4050	8 (5700)	1	16.08.0
Estate of Young Colvills	80	100					0.15.0
A.M. Coffey	46	600				1	1.27.5
William H. Deadrich	240	2600	2 lots	900	2 (900)		6.60.0
John D.A. Daidson						1	0.37.5
Dimmon Dorsey	320	1400					2.10.0
Oliver Dodson	220	1500				1	2.62.5
John Dorsey						1	0.37.5
William E. Dodson						1	0.37.5
Dixon, John G.	10	40				1	0.47.5
Mathew Davis (51)	300	2000			6 (3900)		8.85.0
John G. Dorin (*)			1 lot	600		1	2.55.0
A.P. Fore (PC)	240	2500			7 (3800)		9.90.0
James H. Fyffe	112	637	2 lots	2300	3 (1675)	1	7.29.5
John K. Farmer			2.25 lots	1100		1	2.02.5
Bennet Franklin						1	0.37.5
Jacob Fisher	3	700	1 lot	150			1.27.5
Augustus Fisher						1	0.37.5
Joseph England						1	0.37.5
James Earles			2 lots	400			0.60.0
E.C. Edward						1	0.37.5
Graham Murrell	245	1500					2.25.0
John M. Gibbs (*)			1 lot	800		1	3.15.0
James Gettys	40	700	11 lots	1820	2 (1000)	1	5.65.5
Job Hiatt			1 lot	400			0.60.0
John Howard (52)	320	3500			1 (500)	1	4.87.5
Andrew Hutsel	160	1200				1	2.17.5
James Hemphill						1	0.37.5
Thomas Hopkins heirs			1 lot	400		1	0.60.0
Hilton Humphrey	8	1000				1	1.87.5
George Horne			1 lot	3000		1	4.87.5
Henry Henniger						1	0.37.5
Elijah Hunt/Hand			2 lots	400			0.60.0
John B. Jackson			1 lot	100	1 (500)	1	1.27.5
Urial Johnson	45	200	1 lot	1200	2 (1600)	1	4.87.5
Richard C. Jackson			1 lot	150		1	0.60.0
Theodoro P. Johnson			3 lots	2025		1	3.41.75

Name							
Samuel H. Jordan						1	0.37.5
Charles F. Keith	815	13175			12(6600)		29.66.5
Alexander Keith						1	0.37.5
Peter Kinder (53)	20	250	2 lots	3500			5.62.5
Francis Kindrick	80	350					0.52.5
Pleasant M. Kennedy						1	0.37.5
Richard Kelly	5	150				1	0.60.0
A. D. Keys			2 lots	1000		1	1.87.5
William King	160	600				1	1.27.5
John B. King			0.5 lot	75			0.11.25
Samuel Lotspeich						1	0.37.5
Barthy H. Lowry						1	0.37.5
James Loyd						1	0.37.5
John W. Loyd	160	1000			4 (2800)	1	6.07.5
William Lowry (PC)	750	10000	1 lot	50	7 (4000)	1	21.75.0
Miller Ripley & Co	320	6000					9.00.0
Estate Aaron Mathews	300	2500					3.75.0
Meridian Sun Lodge			0.5 lot	75			0.11.25
Penelope & William Mayfield (54)	480	3200			8 (3100)	1	9.82.5
A. M. McKeldin & Co			2 lots	2000		1	3.37.5
John McGahy					1 (400)	1	0.97.5
Robert McGahy						1	0.37.5
David Moss	160	500				1	1.12.25
Edmund Moss	160	600				1	1.27.5
O.G. Murrill	40	120	2 lots	30075	2 (900)	1	6.51.25
John Moss	440	3500			3 (2400)	1	9.22.5
John Miller	160	500					0.75.0
George W. Major/Marr	4	200	1.5 lots	2475		1	4.38.75
Charles Matlock	160	400					0.60.0
Morrison			1 lot	500		1	1.12.5
Bazel C. Neill						1	0.37.5
Peter A. Neill						1	0.37.5
James Newland	320	2000			1 (700)		4.15.0
Bennet Normon (55)						1	0.37.5
Christen Peters						1	0.37.5
David Pearce	490	2500					3.75.0
Landern C. Peters	240	3500					5.25.0
James Parkison						1	0.37.5
Boyd Porter (*)			1 lot	400			1.20.0

William P. Riggins						1	0.37.5
Jacob Ragsdale						1	0.37.5
Sarah Rudd	160	1200			4 (1800)		4.50.0
Thomas Rudd						1	0.37.5
William Rudd	145	600				1	1.27.5
James T. Reid						1	0.37.5
Joseph Roberson	320	1600			4 (1750)	1	5.40.0
William P. Reid	213.5	900				1	1.72.5
Humphrey Reynolds	240	900					1.35.0
Montreville Reynolds						1	0.37.5
Joseph Rudd (56)	80	350			1 (1000)		2.02.5
Benjamin Ragsdale			2.5 lots	1650		1	2.85.0
Joseph Russel			2 lots	500			0.75.0
James Steed Sr	155	1500					2.25.0
George Sehorn	0.25	600				1	1.27.5
D & M Shield & Co			0.5	1000			1.50.0
John Steed						1	0.37.5
Henry Steed						1	0.37.5
James Steed Jr.						1	0.37.5
Abraham Slover	80	450				1	1.05.0
Samuel Sample	155	800					1.20.0
Estate Benjamin Stout			2 lots	100			0.15.0
Nat Smith	175	975	6 lots	1850			4.23.75
Charles P. Samuel (PC)						1	0.61.5
Ephraim Sautelt/Santell	8	150	1 lot	350		1	1.12.5
William Shook Jr. (57)						1	0.37.5
William Shook Sr.	2	25				1	0.41.25
Isaac Shook	1.5	150				1	0.60.0
Nathan Sullins	160	400	0.5 lot	800		1	0.60.0
P.T. Trotter (*)			0.5 lot	800		1	2.77.5
Joel Triplet	177	1000			1 (500)		2.25.0
Harris D. Thorpe						1	0.37.5
A.B. Thompson	65	200				1	0.67.5
Samuel Workman			1 lot	150		1	0.60.0
David C. Wasson	90	500				1	1.12.5
William Wasson	80	500					0.75.0
Reubin Wilkins	152	400				1	0.97.5
Hiram Worly	160	1100	2 lots	900	1 (800)	1	4.42.5
Thomas Wakefield (58)	80	500				1	1.12.5
James White			4 lots	14000			21.0.0

Name	Acres	Value	2 lots	1000			1	Tax
Alexander Woodward(*)			2 lots	1000			1	3.75.0
Emily S. Walker	1.5	600				1 (700)		1.95.0
Mrs. Youry/Yourg			2 lots	130				0.19.5
T. Nixon Vandyke	80	300	2 lots	1000			1	2.32.5
Tom Weise			1 lot	200				0.30.0

Total Taxpayers: 158, Slaves: 106, Taxes Collected: $392.15.5

1836 TAX LIST - DISTRICT 8

NAME	ACRES	VALUE LAND	SCHOOL	VALUE	SLAVES 12 to 50	WP	TOTAL TAX
Alexander, J.F. (59)	80	100				1	0.52.5
Armstrong, Elihu						1	0.37.5
Autrey, Readicke						1	0.37.5
Autrey, Stephen						1	0.37.5
Bogart, Solomon			160	100			0.15.0
Browder, John W.	80	100					0.15.0
Blankinship, John	93	300				1	0.82.5
Blankinship, Inda	40	20					0.03.0
Beaver, Benjamin						1	0.37.5
Baker, Benjamin M.						1	0.37.5
Beaver, John						1	0.37.5
Beaver, Hyram						1	0.37.5
Beaver, John						1	0.37.5
Brown, Hutson						1	0.37.5
Barns, Pleasant	160	1000				1	1.87.5
Bryant, William (60)	310	1500			1 (500)	1	3.37.5
Blankinship, Isom						1	0.37.5
Broyls, Cornelius						1	0.37.5
Billingsly, Walter	50	120				1	0.18.75
Billingsly, E.H.						1	0.37.5
Billingsly, James	315	500				1	1.12.5
Bedford, Stephen	580	2160			1 (500)	1	4.87.5
Butler, Andrew					1 (500)	1	1.12.5
Browder, S.E.			160	125	1 (500)	1	1.18.75
Cate, John E.	80	800				1	1.57.5

Name							
Cate, William Sr.	220	1600			1 (500)		3.15.0
Cate, William Jr.	200	1200				1	2.17.5
Cate, Charles	100	1100				1	2.02.5
Cash, Thomas						1	0.37.5
Coffman, James						1	0.37.5
Cate, James (61)						1	0.37.5
Cook, Abraham			80	150			0.22.5
Casteel, Alexander	80	100				1	0.52.5
Coxey, Absalem	25	250					0.37.5
Colier, Thomas	110	400				1	0.82.5
Cantrell, Nimrod	320	250	80	10			0.39.0
Caisy/Cains, John	160	200					0.30.0
Dodson, William	75	400				1	0.97.5
Dodson, Warren	120	300				1	0.82.5
Dodson, Henry	160	500				1	1.12.5
Dennis, Allen	280	1000					1.50.0
Dickard, John						1	0.37.5
Dickinson, John	70	250				1	0.75.0
Davis, Anthony	240	1000				1	1.87.5
Daniel, Coleman			100	150		1	0.60.0
Erskin, Hugh (62)						1	0.37.5
Erixon, John						1	0.37.5
Elder, John S.	300	800			1 (300)	1	2.02.5
Ellis, John						1	0.37.5
Essperson, John						1	0.37.5
Franklin, John						1	0.37.5
Franklin, William						1	0.37.5
Franklin, Robert						1	0.37.5
Freeze, Martin			200	300		1	0.82.5
Flanigan, James			160	400		1	0.97.5
Grisham, Elijah	220	800					1.20.0
Gass, Allen G.	80	580	33.3	20		1	1.27.5
Gibson, John			100	300			0.45.0
Grisham, Jesse	320	1200					1.80.0
Gregory, Tapley	220	1000	80	100		1	2.02.5
Gastin, Joseph (63)	290	1400	160	100		1	2.62.5
Hayes, James	160	250				1	0.75.0
Hail, Martin	165	450	160	150		1	1.27.5
Hail, Lewis						1	0.37.5
Hail, James						1	0.37.5

Name							
Harkrider, John	240	400				1	0.97.5
Hays, Solomon	480	400					0.60.0
Hix, Charles						1	0.37.5
Horton, Daniel	191	600				1	1.27.5
Hood, Arthur	74	150					0.22.5
Hunt, L.L.						1	0.37.5
Hentz, A.H.						1	0.37.5
Heaftey, Cornelius	510	1200	240	325	2 (1200)	1	4.46.25
Helvey, Daniel U.						1	0.37.5
Haggard, Richard						1	0.37.5
Henly, James D. (64)	180	800	80	50			1.27.5
Havens, Hiram						1	0.37.5
Hickman, John	160	300				1	0.82.5
Horkeman/Hickman, William						1	0.37.5
Hambrie, Jeremiah	320	1000				1	1.87.5
Helvey, Andrew	80	500				1	1.12.5
Kelly, William						1	0.37.5
Luallen, Jesse	80	200					0.30.0
Luallen, Robert						1	0.37.5
Long, Jesse						1	0.37.5
Large, Isaac						1	0.37.5
Leg, Samuel	160	1400	160	100			2.25.0
Lane, Pleasant W.	225	800			1 (800)	1	2.77.5
Lane, Lidenae	1000	5000			1 (500)	1	8.62.5
Mansel, Robert	244	1200				1	2.17.5
Mansel, Martha (65)	110	420	60	30			0.67.5
Marshall, William						1	0.37.5
McCann, James	72	450					0.67.5
Marlow, George	220	300	420	200		1	1.12.5
McDaniel, Charles W.	111	800			1 (600)	1	2.47.5
McRoy, Thomas						1	0.37.5
McRoy, A.						1	0.37.5
McNabb, William	80	500				1	1.12.5
McNabb, James			80	20		1	0.40.5
Madden, William						1	0.37.5
Moore, Richard	207	450				1	1.05.0
Moore, David			40	50			0.07.5
Newman, John						1	0.37.5
Newman, Alfred C.						1	0.37.5

Name						
Newman, David	340	1300				1.95.0
Newman, William (66)					1	0.37.5
Norman, William	160	400				0.60.0
Owens, Enoch	80	500			1	1.12.5
Price, Charles			160	250	1	0.75.0
Price, John W.					1	0.37.5
Perren, Judah B.F.			300	45		0.45.0
Porter, John R.	160	500			1	1.12.5
Pearce, John					1	0.37.5
Prewit, Richard	80	50			1	0.45.0
Porter, Boyd	240	1000			1	1.87.5
Powell, Scott	155.5	450			1	1.05.0
Roberts, Thomas M.	90	700			1	1.42.0
Roberts, Edmund W.	72	450	150	150	1	1.27.5
Roberts, Edmund	74	400				0.60.0
Riggins, William	160	200			1	0.67.5
Richardson, William(67)	244	1000	80	50		1.57.5
Riggins, Thomas	160	1920	80	80	1	3.37.5
Rice, Jesse	80	150			1	0.60.0
Redferen, Hauzie					1	0.37.5
Rucker, Modica	230	1200			1	2.17.5
Rice, John	80	125			1	0.56.25
Runnels, Daniel					1	0.37.5
Randolph, Robt.	31	200			1	0.67.5
Shelton, William	135	800			1	1.57.5
Shelton, Joseph					1	0.37.5
Shelton, David	150	300	20	50		0.52.5
Shafer, Merideth					1	0.37.5
Shefflet, Austin	177	500			1	1.12.5
Shirrell, Elie	80	250			1	0.75.0
Shell, Benjamin					1	0.37.5
School, John (68)					1	0.37.5
Stout, Daniel					1	0.37.5
Slack, Abram L.	397	3000			1	4.87.5
Shafer, William					1	0.37.5
Spearman, Thomas	200	600			1	1.27.5
Stewart, David			360	200	1	0.67.5
Stokes, Edward S.			215	250	1	0.75.0
Sullins, Nathan	616	3600				5.40.0
Thompson, John C.					1	0.37.5

Name	Acres	Value	School Land	Value	Slaves	WP	Total Tax
Tallent, James						1	0.37.5
Tucker, Thomas						1	0.37.5
Tribble, Stephen						1	0.37.5
Vance, Robert	160	400					0.60.0
Vicon, Thomas	160	900					1.35.0
Wright, Willis	380	1400				1	2.47.5
Womac, Daniel (69)	160	200				1	0.67.5
Womac, Jacob	236	1000			6 (2400)		5.10.0
Ward, Benjamin			240	300		1	0.82.5
White, Obadiah	200	800				1	1.57.5
Witt, James						1	0.37.5
Witt, Silas						1	0.37.5
Witt, Mary	160	800					1.20.0
Williams, John						1	0.37.5
Witt, Joseph	80	500				1	1.12.5
Young, John	80	150				1	0.60.0
Zeigler, Rachel	160	250			1 (500)		1.12.5
Zeigler, Michael						1	0.37.5

Total Taxpayers: 162, Slaves: 18, Taxes Collected: $164.40

1836 TAX LIST - DISTRICT 9

NAME	ACRES	VALUE	SCHOOL LAND	VALUE	SLAVES 12 to 50	WP	TOTAL TAX
John Atkinson (70)	180	1250	40	5	2 (700)	1	3.30.75
Henry Atkinson			80	75		1	0.48.75
John Allen						1	0.37.5
Henry Bess	80	200	40	20			0.33.0
Samuel J. Blackwell						1	0.37.5
Erekiel Bonner	240	1900	160	100	4 (2000)		6.00.0
Moses Bonner						1	0.37.5
James Bonner	160	700			1 (500)	1	2.17.5
Gannon Bradshaw						1	0.37.5
Leuen L. Ball	160	1450	160	50		1	2.62.5
Absalom Coxey	180	550					0.82.5
William Cain						1	0.37.5
Robert Cain						1	0.37.5
Isaac Cain						1	0.37.5

Name							
George Coxey						1	0.37.5
John Erwin (71)						1	0.37.5
James Erwin	100	300				1	0.82.5
Jeremiah Farris	160	200				1	0.67.5
Stephen Farris	80	300					0.45.0
Frederick Foster						1	0.37.5
Joshua Gwinn	80	500			1 (400)	1	1.72.5
Daniel Fitzjarrel	160	150					0.22.5
Asa Fjarrel	40	50				1	0.45.0
Christopher Graves	1000				3 (1600)	1	2.77.5
Archibald Fjarril	100	400				1	0.97.5
John Hardwick	176	1105	160	100	4 (2000)	1	5.18.75
Charles Hardwick						1	0.37.5
William Henderson			40	40			0.06.0
George Henderson						1	0.37.5
Solomon Hardin	170	400					0.60.0
William Hunter (72)			240	150			0.22.5
William Harden						1	0.37.5
Elie Harden						1	0.37.5
James & Aaron Haynes	370	1500					2.25.0
Zachariah Hampton			160	50			0.07.5
Emanuel Haney	320	1400			1 (500)	1	3.22.5
Willis Haney						1	0.37.5
George M. Haynes			120	10			0.01.5
James Hawkins	120	400					0.60.0
Andrew Hooper	120	200					0.30.0
John Johnson			150	100			0.15.0
Elizabeth Jamison			80	46			0.06.75
Benjamin C. Jamison			130	75		1	0.48.75
James Isom						1	0.37.5
John Kibble			160	100			0.15.0
William Kean/Kear (73)	120	150	160	300			0.67.5
John Leadbetter						1	0.37.5
John M. Love	158	230	20	20		1	0.75.0
Hardy S. Morris	400	1450	80	50			2.25.0
Thomas Mcinturff			80	80		1	0.49.5
Benj. Newton	310	900	320	175			1.61.25
Thomas Newton						1	0.37.5
William Night						1	0.37.5
Levi Only	188	230	20	20		1	0.75.0

Name							
Robert Philips	182	450				1	1.05.0
John Pugh	320	1500					2.25.0
Hiram Pugh						1	0.37.5
Jonathan Pugh						1	0.37.5
Sarah Pugh	160	150					0.22.5
Sirus Quiott	40	80				1	0.49.5
Robert Collins (74)	160	500				1	1.12.5
George W. Roper						1	0.37.5
John M. Roper	160	300	160	100		1	0.97.5
Joseph Rhinehart			200	150			0.22.5
Michel Robinet			190	200			0.30.0
Zadock Richardson						1	0.37.5
Nancy Ramsey			160	100			0.15.0
John Stanfield	80	200				1	0.67.5
Robert Sharp						1	0.37.5
Coonrod Stainer	240	400	120	75		1	1.08.75
Hamilton Stewart	320	1000	240	200		1	2.17.5
Lucy Stepp	80	150					0.22.5
Henry R. Stokes	160	160					0.24.0
George A. Shield	160	300					0.45.0
James Sewell	250	200					0.30.0
George Sewell (75)						1	0.37.5
Jackson Sewell						1	0.37.5
Hiram Sharp					1 (700)	1	1.42.5
Joel Sharp	140	80	120	80	1 (500)	1	1.36.5
Jacob Sharp	302	1500	40	5	1 (500)		3.00.75
Wallace W. Sevils	163	125	866	107		1	0.72.25
James Shelton	602	1660				1	2.86.5
Sylvanus Stokes			280	600		1	1.27.5
James Seaborn	200	900				1	1.72.5
James Stewart						1	0.37.5
John Seaborn	200	500	215	300		1	1.57.5
Thomas Smart	640	1700	140	200	1 (500)		3.60.0
Francis Triplin						1	0.37.5
William Tallent						1	0.37.5
Edmund Walker						1	0.37.5
James E. Walker (76)						1	0.37.5
William Walker	160	500				1	1.12.5
Robert Walker	320	1200					1.80.0
James Walker	40	1250				1	0.39.0

Name	Acres	Value					Total Tax
John S. Wooten						1	0.37.5
John Walker	80	150	120	10			0.24.0
James Wood			90	80		1	0.49.0
William Zeigler	133	700					1.05.0

Total Taxpayers: 99, Slaves: 20, Taxes Collected: $90.47.75

1836 TAX LIST - DISTRICT 10

NAME	ACRES	VALUE LAND	SCHOOL	VALUE	SLAVES 12 to 50	WP	TOTAL TAX
Allen, William (77)	160	400				1	0.97.5
Armsted, William	160	75					0.11.25
Allen, Archibald B.						1	0.37.5
Atkinson, John	160	200				1	0.30.0
Blair, William	80	300				1	0.82.5
Binton/Benton, Thomas	90	200					0.30.0
Bogart, Solomon	80	40					0.06.0
Brumfield, Medad						1	0.37.5
Blair, John						1	0.37.5
Crow, Denson						1	0.37.5
Carnes, John	160	400				1	0.97.5
Crownover, Benj.	113	350					0.52.5
Cowan, James Jr.	180	800				1	1.57.5
Combs, Elizabeth	160	200					0.30.0
Couch, Jonathan	160	1000				1	1.87.25
Cunningham, Saml.B.(78)	160	350	80	50		1	0.97.5
Cowan, James Sr.	330	500					0.75.0
Caldwell, Thomas	224	1200					1.80.0
Combs, Auborn	170	150				1	0.60.0
Charles, McConnall						1	0.37.5
Dugan, Thomas						1	0.37.5
Dodson, Jesse						1	0.37.5
Dodson, Elisha	387	2777	80	80	1 (500)	1	5.41.0
Dodson, Jesse	297	1300				1	2.32.5
Dodson, Nimrod						1	0.37.5
Dickerson, Charles						1	0.37.5

Name							
Edens, Archibald	320	1500				1	2.62.5
Fisher, John B						1	0.37.5
Forrist, William L.						1	0.37.5
Gilliland, Daniel						1	0.37.5
Gibson, Mathew R. (79)	130	700				1	1.42.5
HarkRider, George						1	0.37.5
Huffaker, James	160	600				1	1.27.5
Hunt, John						1	0.37.5
Hicky, James	734	3150			2 (1000)	1	6.60.0
Hamilton, Joshua	80	400				1	0.97.5
Hicks, Abraham						1	0.37.5
Haney, Emanuel	164	600				1	1.27.5
Hicklen, Barney						1	0.37.5
Ingram, George						1	0.37.5
Johnson, William	160	600					0.90.0
Jerrel, John F.			80	100			0.15.0
Jones, William						1	0.37.5
Johnson, William						1	0.37.5
Kinmon, Samuel	320	500					0.75.0
Kinmon, William (80)						1	0.37.5
Kinser, Henry						1	0.37.5
King, Henry						1	0.37.5
Laird, Samuel						1	0.37.5
Laird, Joseph						1	0.37.5
Langley, Jonathan	140	600				1	1.27.5
Laird, David						1	0.37.5
McNabb, James	350	1500				1	2.62.5
Madden, James						1	0.37.5
Murphrey, John M.	200	800					1.20.0
Murphrey, William						1	0.37.5
Misier, Elijah						1	0.37.5
Melton, Burrell						1	0.37.5
Moody, Joseph C.						1	0.37.5
Miller, Thomas	220	2500	40	5		1	4.13.25
McCarty, John L. (81)	640	2400					3.60.0
McCamman, Elizabeth C.	520	2500			7 (2550)		7.42.5
McCully, Joseph						1	0.37.5
Morton, Silas			80	175		1	0.63.75
McCully, George	160	500				1	1.12.5
Melton, Carter	401	2100					3.15.0

Name							
Maxfield, Benjamin	440	2250			3 (1100)	1	5.40.0
Moody, Andrew J.						1	0.37.5
Matlock, John	500	2675			4 (2700)	1	8.43.75
Musie/Music, John	170	800					1.20.0
Mitchel, Allen						1	0.37.5
Mcanally, Charles						1	0.37.5
Napier, A.H.			70	150			0.22.5
Orton, James	80	400				1	0.97.5
Overby, Hiram						1	0.37.5
Pike, James H. (82)						1	0.37.5
Pike, John B.						1	0.37.5
Peak, Bluford						1	0.37.5
Peak, Shel	160	350					0.52.5
Pettit, Francis						1	0.37.5
Parkison, Manuel	720	3240	180	360			5.40.0
Parkison, Thomas	160	1000					1.50.0
Parkison, John						1	0.37.5
Porter, William B.	330	1500			3 (1500)	1	4.87.5
Parson, William						1	0.37.5
Quck, John						1	0.37.5
Richardson, James						1	0.37.5
Rentfro, Robert	720	4000			4 (1600)	1	8.77.5
Richardson, Samuel	135	125				1	0.56.25
Roberts, George					3 (1500)		2.25.0
Reece, Elijah (83)	50	50					0.07.5
Reece, Isaac	400	2500				1	11.12.5
Reece, John	166	1200			2 (800)	1	3.37.5
Robinet, Michel	160	400				1	0.97.5
Rucker, James	280	2000					4.50.0
Rice, Charles W.	160	1700	120	120		1	3.10.5
Rice, Lani S.						1	0.37.5
Sisk, Alexander						1	0.37.5
Sevils, Absalem	44	130				1	0.57.0
Senter, Martin	340	2000				1	3.37.5
Stewart, David	160	400					0.60.0
Stewart, John D.						1	0.37.5
Scarborough, Jas.						1	0.37.5
Spearman, Wesley	280	800				1	1.57.5
Smith, James						1	0.37.5
Smith, Isaac (84)						1	0.37.5

Name	Acres	Value			Slaves	WP	Total Tax
Shugart, John C.						1	0.37.5
Taylor, Larkin	160	1200				1	2.17.5
Tallant, Maliki						1	0.37.5
Ward, Ezekiel						1	0.37.5
Williams, William						1	0.37.5
Waters, Isaac						1	0.37.5
Wasson, Benjamin	580	2000				1	3.3.75
Wolf, Daniel						1	0.37.5
Waters, Moses	160	250					0.37.5
Young, John F.						1	0.37.5

Total Taxpayers: 116, Slaves: 29, Taxes Collected: $150.11.25

1836 TAX LIST - DISTRICT 11

NAME	ACRES	VALUE LAND	SCHOOL	VALUE	SLAVES 12 to 50	WP	TOTAL TAX
Albert Largent/Sargent	100	300				1	0.82.5
Andrew Burk (85)	268	2500				1	4.12.5
Absalem Wilson	80	500				1	1.12.5
Allen Weise	120	500				1	1.12.5
Allen Craig						1	0.37.5
Adolphus Gamble	50	500				1	1.12.5
Archibald Hail						1	0.37.5
A.H. Napier	180	600					0.90.0
Andrew Cowan	213	1000				1	1.87.5
Allen Armstrong	140	500					0.75.0
Absalem Hays						1	0.37.5
Alexander Roberson	180	3000			1 (600)		5.40.0
Bannister Colier						1	0.37.5
Birden McCoy	80	200					0.30.0
B.R. Bingham	60	50				1	0.45.0
Barnacus McKiney (86)	158	300				1	0.82.5
Benjamin Right						1	0.37.5
Charles W. Medaras						1	0.37.5
Caswell Jonigan	270	1500				1	2.62.25
Chrisley Baker	64	200					0.30.0
Clem Eaton						1	0.37.5

Name					
Caleb Haymes	80	300		1	0.82.5
Coonrod Miller				1	0.37.5
Daniel Richards	160	500		1	0.75.0
Daniel Pierce	125	500		1	1.12.5
Daniel Haymes				1	0.37.5
David Greinway				1	0.37.5
David Haymes				1	0.37.5
Ephraim Maples	200	600		1	1.27.5
Elihu Boberson				1	0.37.5
Ephram Witt (87)				1	0.37.5
Elizabeth McMahan	320	1000			1.50.0
Fletcher Strange	80	300			0.82.0
Frederick Hail	80	350		1	0.90.0
Fleming Gibbs				1	0.37.5
Granderson Hunt				1	0.37.5
George Trotter	45	100		1	0.52.5
George Parker				1	0.37.5
Hugh Mcdonald				1	0.37.5
Herny Hamilton				1	0.37.5
Hezekiah Angel	53	200		1	0.67.5
Hugh P. Wilson	792	1000		1	1.87.5
Hugh Johns				1	0.37.5
Henry Walker	200	1000	1 (700)	1	2.92.5
Hudson Johnson				1	0.37.5
Hugh Larimore (88)	160	700			1.05.0
Isham Thompson				1	0.37.5
Isham Prince				1	0.37.5
Isarah Davis				1	0.37.5
Isaac Shirell	80	300		1	0.82.5
John Thompson	126	500		1	1.12.5
John Templeton Jr.	90	600			0.90.0
James Colier	63	500		1	0.82.5
Jesse Blackburn	216	500		1	1.12.5
John Mederis				1	0.37.5
James Griffin				1	0.37.5
John Williams	80	300		1	0.82.5
John Blackburn				1	0.37.5
Jarrett Johnson				1	0.37.5
James Wallin	185	800		1	1.67.5
Jesse Hinkle (89)	102	500		1	0.82.5

Name					
John Brookshear				1	0.37.5
John Neal	117	500		1	0.82.5
John Crump				1	0.37.5
Joseph Culwell	50	200		1	0.67.5
John A. Tompson	110	500		1	1.12.5
John Mcdonal	160	300		1	0.82.5
John Davis				1	0.37.5
James Wilson	370	1100		1	2.02.5
John Gibson	160	700		1	1.42.5
Joshua Haymes	70	100			0.15.0
Jonathan Cry				1	0.37.5
John Boatman				1	0.37.5
John Davis				1	0.37.5
Joll Pettett				1	0.37.5
Joseph Black (90)	137	300			0.45.0
John Newman				1	0.37.5
Jane Haymes			1 (400)		0.60.0
James Julian	200	900		1	1.72.5
James Casada				1	0.37.5
Jesse Dodson	100	400		1	0.97.5
John Ghee				1	0.37.5
John Lang	115	800		1	1.57.5
John Burk				1	0.37.5
James Pearce	480	3000		1	4.87.5
Jacob Basinger				1	0.37.5
John Miller	168	600		1	1.27.5
John Beler	160	2000		1	3.37.5
Juliet Thomas	79	450		1	1.05.0
Josiah Markham				1	0.37.5
John Baker (91)	238	1600		1	2.77.5
Lowry Smith	147	300		1	0.82.5
Little Bury Moore	290	1550		1	2.70.0
Lazeraus Chitwood	160	300			0.45.0
Levie Dodson				1	0.37.5
Malcom McDeugal	159	1000	1 (600)		2.40.0
Martin Casada	240	1200			1.80.0
Manuel Shote/Scott				1	0.37.5
Martin Frazure	100	450		1	1.05.0
Maize Blackburn	150	800	2 (1400)	1	3.67.5
Nicholas Dodson	560	2500		1	4.12.5

Name					
Nimrod Triplet	122	700		1	1.42.5
Nathaniel Crittendon	120	200		1	0.67.5
Robt. Barnett	140	500		1	1.12.5
Reuben Longwitt				1	0.37.5
Richard Been (92)				1	0.37.5
Robt. B. Caldwell				1	0.37.5
Robt. Hamilton				1	0.37.5
Robt. Lacky				1	0.37.5
Robt. McNight	160	400			0.60.0
Russel Smith	160	550		1	1.20.0
Roland Laramore	40	40		1	0.43.5
Samuel W. Thompson				1	0.37.5
Syrus Green				1	0.37.5
Solomon Easters				1	0.37.5
Samuel Patterson	158	500	3 (1130)	1	2.82.0
Sarah Williams	80	200			0.70.0
Stephen Wells				1	0.37.5
Samuel Frazure				1	0.37.5
Samuel Barnett	89	400		1	0.97.5
Samuel Combs (93)				1	0.37.5
Thos. Becket				1	0.37.5
Thos Maples				1	0.37.5
Vincent Woods				1	0.37.5
Vincent Haymes	170	800	1 (350)	1	2.10.0
Willeford Chapman				1	0.37.5
William Medarias				1	0.37.5
William Griffin	115	200			0.30.0
Wm. B. Caldwell				1	0.37.5
Wm. B. Hays	65	200		1	0.67.5
Wm. C. Gibson				1	0.37.5
Williamson Thompson	200	800		1	1.57.5
Wm. McKenny				1	0.37.5
Wm. Burk	452	1500		1	2.62.5
Wm. Whittle				1	0.37.5
William Emerson (94)	180	800	1 (600)	1	2.47.5
William R. Duglas	160	500		1	0.82.5
William W. Moore				1	0.37.5
William W. Smith	200	1000		1	1.87.5
William Randolph	44	250		1	0.75.0
William Haymes				1	0.37.5

Name	Acres	Value				WP	Total
William Casida						1	0.37.5
William Anderson	107	250					0.37.5
William H. Dearick	320	1200					1.80.0
Walter K. Nicholas						1	0.37.5
James Hand	160	300				1	0.82.5
Ardel Harden						1	0.37.5
Easter Samuel	180	600					0.60.0
Nathan Stafford						1	0.37.5
Joseph Stafford						1	0.37.5
Western Peace (95)	160	500				1	1.12.5
William Moss	80	300				1	0.82.5
Young H. Griffin						1	0.37.5
Steven Jones	582	3000				1	4.87.5

Total Taxpayers: 154, Slaves: 11, Taxes Collected: $146.40.5

1836 TAX LIST - DISTRICT 12

NAME	ACRES	VALUE LAND	SCHOOL	VALUE	SLAVES 12 to 50	WP	TOTAL TAX
Armstrong, Absalom(96)	160	1000				1	1.77.5
Armstrong, Allen	160	1000				1	1.87.5
Armstrong, Andrew	320	1500				1	2.62.5
Armstrong, Casey	160	300				1	0.82.5
Armstrong, Clinton						1	0.37.5
Armstrong, William Jr.	80	400			1 (400)	1	1.57.5
Armstrong, John	150	800			4 (1200)	1	3.37.5
Armstrong, Wm. P.						1	0.37.5
Armstrong, James						1	0.37.5
Armstrong, Thomas	240	1600			4 (1400)		4.50.0
Armstrong, William Sr.	315	1400			4 (1400)		4.20.0
Armstrong, Baker						1	0.37.5
Armstrong, Samuel						1	0.37.5
Bogart, Solomon	330	1200					1.80.0
Bivem/Bowen, Joseph						1	0.37.5
Boon, Israel (97)	160	150					0.22.5
Barnes/Burns, Susanah			80	80			0.12.0
Brown, William	400	800					1.20.0
Brown, Joseph						1	0.37.5

Name							
Burgen, Adam						1	0.37.5
Burns, John						1	0.37.5
Biler, John	320	1200			1 (500)	1	2.92.5
Bloom, E.P.	160	800				1	1.57.5
Bailey, James	80	450				1	1.05.0
Cox, James	50	300				1	0.82.5
Chesnut, James	160	1000				1	1.87.5
Crocket, John A.						1	0.37.5
Chesnut, Raleigh	220	1000				1	1.87.5
Cantrell, John M.	80	117				1	0.55.25
Caldwell, Andrew	160	700				1	1.42.5
Copeland, John (98)	80	400			1 (500)	1	1.72.5
Carlock, Isaac	80	200					0.30.0
Copeland, Alexander	80	400			1 (400)	1	1.57.5
Carouth, Walley	320	1000				1	1.87.5
Cantrell, Elijah	120	300				1	0.82.5
Cantrell, Gabriel	188	1000				1	1.87.5
Clark, Alfred L.						1	0.37.5
Cantrell, David	195	1600				1	2.77.5
Cantrell, Jacob	47.5	100				1	0.52.5
Crocket, John	320	1500					2.25.0
Chapmon, E.W.	80	300				1	0.82.5
Copeland, Joseph					1 (800)	1	1.57.5
Cate, Gideon	200	1000			1 (500)	1	2.62.5
Cantrell, Isaac	233	800				1	1.57.5
Cantrell, Wm.	80	117				1	0.55.25
Caues/Cave, William(99)						1	0.37.5
Carlock, Jas. C.	80	250				1	0.75.0
Duckworth, John	53	270				1	0.78.0
Duckworth, Saml.	80	250					0.37.5
Derick, Michel	370	1300					1.95.0
Derick, Jacob L.						1	0.37.5
Dugan, William						1	0.37.5
Dorsey, Dimon	160	800				1	1.57.5
Derick, John	110	350				1	0.90.0
Fore, A.P.	240	700					1.05.0
Firestone, D.S.	160	200	160	25		1	0.71.25
Fenneel, J.B.						1	0.37.5
Ferguson, Wm.	320	1000				1	1.87.5
Firestone, Wm.						1	0.37.5

Name							
Firestone, Alfred						1	0.37.5
Foster, Simpson (100)						1	0.37.5
Firestone, Samuel	240	300	80	40			0.51.0
Firestone, Mathias	629	1500					2.25.0
Fann, Malcath					2 (500)		0.75.0
Fann, Caleb						1	0.37.5
Fite, Peter Sr.	320	1500			1 (300)		2.70.0
Fite, Henry						1	0.37.5
Fite, Elias						1	0.37.5
Fite, Peter Jr.						1	0.37.5
Foster, Anthony						1	0.37.5
Good, Edward						1	0.37.5
Glase, George H.	76	100				1	0.52.5
Good, John					2 (1000)	1	1.87.5
Grogan, Albert			160	100		1	0.52.5
Griffith, John S.	80	300				1	0.82.5
Glase, William S. (101)						1	0.37.5
Cox, John						1	0.37.5
Cox, Gale						1	0.37.5
Henry, Bartholomew	160	150					0.22.5
Hester, Abraham			160	100		1	0.52.5
Helton, Wiley						1	0.37.5
Hill, John	1000	3000			4 (2400)	1	8.62.5
Jackson, John K.	240	1200				1	2.17.5
Jamison, Thomas						1	0.37.5
Jack, Mary			160	400			0.60.0
Jack, James						1	0.37.5
Long, Samuel	110	400				1	0.97.5
Long, James	337.5	1200				1	2.17.5
Lawson, A.H.						1	0.37.5
Lawson, Isom	190	1000					1.50.0
Lawson, Russel (102)	80	500				1	1.12.5
Lovel, John	80	100					0.15.0
Logan, Abner						1	0.37.5
Masengale, James	20	50					0.07.5
Masengale, Adam G.	116	1000				1	1.87.5
Masten, Reuben	300	1500					2.25.0
Masten, Thomas W.	100	800			1 (500)	1	2.32.5
Morris, John Esq.	535	2500			1 (400)	1	4.72.5
Mayfield, Thomas B.	160	1000			2 (880)	1	3.15.0

Name							
Marten, William	175	450				1	1.05.0
Marten, Samuel	160	800				1	1.57.5
McGhee, Daniel H.					3 (1000)	1	1.87.5
Morris, Stephen						1	0.37.5
Masony/Marony, Samuel						1	0.37.5
Newman, Robert M.	480	4500				1	7.12.5
Newman, William (103)	80	400				1	0.97.5
Newman, James	80	400				1	0.97.5
Norris, West						1	0.37.5
Orr, William	160	800					1.20.0
Owens, John						1	0.37.5
Owens, Thomas						1	0.37.5
Patty, Obed.							
Proffit, Aronton	144	1400				1	2.47.5
Reynold, H. Estate	320	1525	160	75			2.40.0
Reynold, Isaiah	250	1000			1 (500)	1	2.62.5
Roberd/Roper, Joseph L.	50	50					0.07.5
Richard, Sam.	60	100					0.15.0
Reynold, Isaac W.						1	0.37.5
Roberts, Joshua						1	0.37.5
Stephenson, John						1	0.37.5
Stephenson, Robert(104)	269	2000			3 (1000)		4.50.0
Studdard, Thomas					2 (800)	1	1.57.5
Stubblsfield, Robt.	159.5	450				1	1.05
Stubblsfield, Mahala	160	400					0.60.0
Sparks, William						1	0.37.5
Suthard, Reuben P.						1	0.37.5
Smith, Robert	100	185					0.27.75
Smith, Russel	83	150					0.22.5
Simpson, John						1	0.37.5
Smith, Gideon W.						1	0.37.5
Saxon, William Jr.						1	0.37.5
Scott, James	81.75	200				1	0.67.5
Thompson, Daniel	160	400					0.60.0
Thompson, Lemuel Est.	160	500					0.75.0
Thompson, John	210	700				1	1.42.5
Taylor, B.H. (105)	152	500				1	1.12.5
Triplet, Lewis	250	600				1	1.27.5
Wakefield, Charls	177	1000			1 (450)		2.17.5
William, John						1	0.37.5

NAME	ACRES	VALUE	SCHOOL LAND	VALUE	SLAVES 12 to 50	WP	TOTAL TAX
White, Wm. H.	80	350					0.52.5
Wilson, Wm. H.	195	400				1	0.97.5
White, Commadore						1	0.37.5
Wadkins, Wm.			160	100			0.15.0
White, Elizabeth	390	1500					2.25.0
Young, Moses						1	0.37.5
Wakefield, Alexander						1	0.37.5
White, John						1	0.37.5

Total Taxpayers: 145, Slaves: 41, Taxes Collected: $171.08

1836 TAX LIST - DISTRICT 13

NAME	ACRES	VALUE	SCHOOL LAND	VALUE	SLAVES 12 to 50	WP	TOTAL TAX
Barnett, James (106)			160	200			0.30.0
Brock, Elbert						1	0.37.5
Brock, Daniel H.						1	0.37.5
Bowring, Nicholas	139.5	600				1	1.27.5
Benton, Edmond	160	400	120	200			0.90.0
Benton, Jesse H.						1	0.37.5
Bowling, Samuel	160	300					0.45.0
Bowring, Ezekiel						1	0.37.5
Belcher, Noah						1	0.37.5
Brown, Joel K.			1	10			0.01.5
Cloud, Osage	160	150					0.22.5
Cast, John						1	0.37.5
Cast, James			135	200			0.30.0
Carter, Thomas						1	0.37.5
Carter, Frederick						1	0.37.5
Cast, Moses (107)	160	325					0.48.75
Carney, Joshua	160	300					0.45.0
Carney, Madison						1	0.37.5
Carney, George						1	0.37.5
Casteel, Barney	140	300	187	400		1	1.42.5
Carter, Robert						1	0.37.5
Carter, Benjamin						1	0.37.5
Carter, Amos						1	0.37.5

Name							
Cockboan/Cockhorn, John						1	0.37.5
Cast, Benjamin						1	0.37.5
Crawford, John	660	500					0.75.0
Cobb, David A.			600	100			0.15.0
Cook, William H.	560	3700	640	300	4 (2000)		9.00.0
Cooss, Jacob						1	0.37.5
Campbell, Katharine	160	300	160	50			0.52.5
Dilday, Simeon (108)	100	300				1	0.82.5
Dilda, Charles	80	150					0.22.5
Dortherly, Charles			125	300		1	0.82.5
Ditmore, Vincent	380	250	80	50		1	0.82.5
Dortherly, Mathew						1	0.37.5
Dodson, James	156	300					0.45.0
Dodson, John						1	0.37.5
Derick, Michael C.	820	2230				1	3.72.0
Ditmore, John						1	0.37.5
Dearmon, John			120	100			0.15.0
Eller, Joshua	360	1700	120	12		1	2.95.0
Elliott, John						1	0.37.5
Esmon, John						1	0.37.5
Eller, James F.						1	0.37.5
Fore, A.P.	400	100					0.15.0
Gentry, Samuel (109)			50	100		1	0.52.5
Gregory, John	80	80					0.12.0
Hunt, Levi B.	188.5	600				1	1.27.5
Hestor, Abraham			80	25			0.03.75
Hamby, Nedom	120	200					0.30.0
Hamby, Nedom	70	50					0.07.5
Hooper, William	80	250					0.37.5
Jack, John						1	0.37.5
Kelly, Nathan			40	50		1	0.45.0
Kelly, Jonathan			100	200			0.30.0
Kelly, Nathan R.						1	0.37.5
Kelly, William	40	75	120	100			0.26.25
Kelly, Richard			40	40		1	0.43.5
Kelly, Daniel			40	40			0.06.0
Kelly, Samuel			40	60			0.09.0
Lesley, Thomas (110)						1	0.37.5
Lesley, Thomas Sr.	160	600					0.90.0

Name							
Lesley, Samuel			220	300		1	0.82.5
Lowry, Michael	140	200					0.30.0
Langham, Elias	30.5	40					0.06.0
Manery, Edward	80	150				1	0.60.0
Moore, Ransom J.	100	400				1	0.97.5
Moss, Elie						1	0.37.5
Prince, Josiah			120	150			0.22.5
Prince, Wiley			40	60		1	0.46.5
Prince, Andrew J.						1	0.37.5
Pack, George						1	0.37.5
Pack, Thomas						1	0.37.5
Hamby, Adam	60	200					0.30.0
Rice, John	160	200				1	0.67.5
Rutherford, Larken(111)						1	0.37.5
Rainey, John			160	100		1	0.52.5
Ryan, Amos	160	300					0.45.0
Riggs, Samuel						1	0.37.5
Riggs, James J.						1	0.37.5
Chelton, John	160	450	60	30			0.72.5
Stillwill, Jeremiah			320	30			0.04.5
Stambury, Thos.						1	0.37.5
Starr, Caleb	1550	8000			2 (1000)		13.50.0
Thomas, John	84	600				1	1.27.5
Thompson, Robt.	160	200				1	0.67.5
Witt, Hezekiah			160	700		1	1.42.5
Witt, William						1	0.37.5
Witt, Burgess						1	0.37.5
White, Elisha	140	300				1	0.82.5
White, Jesse (112)	260	500			1 (100)	1	1.27.5
White, Daniel	155	400				1	0.97.5
Witt, Valentine						1	0.37.5
Womlite/Womble, William						1	0.37.5
Wadkins, William						1	0.37.5

Total Taxpayers: 95, Slaves: 7, Taxes Collected: $71.94.75

1836 TAX LIST - DISTRICT 14

NAME	ACRES	VALUE LAND	SCHOOL	VALUE	SLAVES 12 to 50	WP	TOTAL TAX
Bayley, John (113)						1	0.37.5
Bunch, Charles						1	0.37.5
Barksdale, Sherrod						1	0.37.5
Bolding, James						1	0.37.5
Barksdale, Allen						1	0.37.5
Bolding, Obadiah	159	600					0.90.0
Bolding, William L.					1 (350)	1	0.90.0
Bookout, Wright						1	0.37.5
Bolding, Collins	160	600					0.90.0
Bogart, Solomon	160	150					0.22.5
Culpepier, Burrel S.						1	0.37.5
Cook, Washing						1	0.37.5
Cameron, Archibald	160	500					0.75.0
Cobles/Cobb, Davis A.	550	3000			1 (1400)	1	6.97.5
Cobles/Cobb, Joseph	480	1500			1 (400)	1	3.22.5
Calhoun, William (114)	160	75				1	0.48.75
Caragan, Marcus						1	0.37.5
Carlock, Isaac	153.5	400					0.60.0
Cameron, William						1	0.37.5
Cook, Hezekiah C.	160	1200				1	2.17.5
Calhoun, James	560	1000					1.50.0
Cooper, John P.						1	0.37.5
Cooper, Henry Est.	540	1000					1.50.0
Coble/Cobb, John	520	1800				1	3.07.5
Cantile, Gabriel			38	20			0.03.0
Dickey, John P.						1	0.37.5
Douglas, James	160	300					0.45.0
Douglas, John	160	1000			2 (900)	1	3.22.5
Dodd, John						1	0.37.5
Divine, John	320	300					0.45.0
Ellis, John J. (115)	100	165			1 (500)	1	1.37.25
Everton, Thomas						1	0.37.5
Farmer, James						1	0.37.5
Firestone, Samuel	320	600			2 (800)	1	2.47.5

Fore, A.P.	1114.5	5000	7 (2950)	11.92.5
Grigg, Joel	100	250	1	0.75.0
Gee, John	173	1000		1.50.0
Gee, Hiram			1	0.37.5
Gilbreath, Thomas			1	0.37.5
Gilbreath, Elizabeth	300	3000	4 (1600)	6.90.0
Green, James S.	160	200	1	0.67.5
Green, Alexander	160	200		0.30.0
Gibbs, John M.	115	300		0.45.0
Gibbs, Richard			1	0.37.5
Howard, Thomas			1	0.37.5
Hoyle, Jonas (116)			1	0.37.5
Hoyle, Peter	292.5	500	1	1.12.5
Huffaker, Benj.			1	0.37.5
Hoyle, John	224	1500	6 (2600)	6.15.0
Hoyle, Thomas L.	480	1500	3 (1500) 1	4.87.5
Hooper, Augustus			1	0.37.5
Harris, George	250	1200	1	2.17.5
Huffaker, Christopher			1	0.37.5
Hardy, William B.	280	300		0.45.0
Hoyle, Andrew	132	200		0.30.0
Hoyle, David	271	1000		1.50.0
Huffaker, Lewis	160	800		1.20.0
Kelly, Samuel	335	900	1	1.72.5
Kerksey, George W.	200	300	1	0.82.5
Kerksey, Thomas	160	250	1	0.75.0
Logan, Elizabeth (117)	160	250		0.37.5
Lingerfelt, Jacob	160	500		0.75.0
Latimore, Susannah	280	1300	2 (700)	3.00.0
Long, Samuel	80	150		0.22.5
Madox, Joseph	160	300		0.45.0
McBrier, William	160	300	1	0.82.5
McGowen, Francis	160	160	1	0.61.5
Maples, William	420	2000	2 (1200)	4.80.0
Madaux, Nathaniel	340	500	1	1.12.5
Nelson, Henry			1	0.37.5
Parris, William	720	1440		2.16.0
Parris, John W.			1	0.37.5
Parris Lemuel			1	0.37.5
Patterson, Wm.	160	500		0.75.0

Payne, Lewis					1 (500)	1	1.12.5
Richey/Ridley, William						1	0.37.5
Reynolds, Green L.(118)	160	600				1	1.27.5
Rheynhart, Lewis	170	400					0.60.0
Roper, Joseph	216	200					0.30.0
Sutterfield, James						1	0.37.5
Seaton, William						1	0.37.5
Sitz, Margaret	100	250					0.37.5
Schelton, Thomas						1	0.37.5
Smith, Robert	60	150					0.22.5
Tinney, Isaac	155	200			1 (800)		1.50.0
Tinney, William						1	0.37.5
Vaughn, Thomas	60	75					0.11.25
Wheeler, Gabrel						1	0.37.5
Wilson, Andrew M.						1	0.37.5
Weatherly, Mary			160	20			0.03.0
Witt, Rutherford (119)	1160	400					0.60.0
Witt, James H.					1 (400)	1	0.87.5
Wells, Thomas P.	280	1500			1 (1200)	1	0.42.5
Weatherly, Jobe						1	0.37.5
Yancy, Maridy						1	0.37.5
Yancy, Alexander						1	0.37.5

Total Taxpayers: 96, Slaves: 36, Taxes Collected: $114.90.75

1836 TAX LIST - DISTRICT 15

NAME	ACRES	VALUE LAND	SCHOOL	VALUE	SLAVES 12 to 50	WP	TOTAL TAX
Allison, William P.(120)	241	1000				1	1.87.5
Atchly, Thomas	140	800					1.20.0
Allen, Lee P.						1	0.37.5
Ash, Robert	160	600					0.90.0
Ash, James R.						1	0.37.5
Alexander, Joseph					2 (1400)	1	2.47.5
Bryant, William	320	320					0.48.0
Brewer, Lewis	154	400				1	1.27.5
Bowerman, John	80	300				1	0.82.5
Barker, Burrel						1	0.37.5
Bigham, Matilda	160	100					0.15.0
Bigham, Mary	47.5	50					0.07.5
Burk, John	160	300					0.45.0
Burk, Jonas M.						1	0.37.5
Baker, James						1	0.37.5
Bailey, James (*)						1	0.37.5
Blair, James (*)						1	0.37.5
Bailey, Sam. P. (*)						1	0.37.5
Bailey, Washington (*)						1	0.37.5
Bivens, Nathaniel (121)	80	200					0.30.0
Barker, Burrel	355	850				1	1.65.0
Basinger, Michael						1	0.37.5
Crabtree, Thomas	80	200				1	0.67.5
Cobles/Cobb,Joseph(PC)	320	1360			3 (1100)		3.78.0
Cox, John	160	500				1	1.12.5
Crittendan, John						1	0.37.5
Caddell, Parson	80	160				1	0.61.5
Conner, John						1	0.37.5
Cash, Howard						1	0.37.5
Campbell, Phebe	160	350					2.05.0
Drake, Siles	86	325			1 (500)		1.23.75
Daughorty, John	160	300					0.45.0
Doan, Ira	261	1000				1	1.87.5
Doan, John						1	0.37.5

Name					
Davis, Isaac	160	500		1	1.12.5
Duthro, Jacob (122)	160	400		1	0.97.5
Elliott, John	181	300			0.45.0
Foggy, James				1	0.37.5
Funkhouser, Jacob	160	200			0.30.0
Grills, Thomas S.	200	1000	1 (600)	1	2.77.5
Gibson, Thomas	220	220			0.33.0
Green, Richard				1	0.37.5
Hardy, Thomas	80	150		1	0.60.0
Harris, John				1	0.37.5
Hanks, John	240	1000		1	1.87.5
Hamby, Jesse (*)					0.75.0
Hamilton, Jesse	160	600	1 (500)	1	1.65.0
Hoss, Jacob (*)	160	100			0.30.0
Hickox, Heirs	260	1600			2.40.0
Hughes, Pryor				1	0.75.0
Iseby, George				1	0.37.5
Jones, Reece	154	300			0.45.0
Jones, Samuel				1	0.37.5
Lemons, Holden (123)				1	0.37.5
Lemons, Reuben				1	0.37.5
Lemons, William	160	500		1	1.12.5
ditto	494	805			1.20.75
Long, Moses	160	800		1	1.57.5
Langly, James	80	400		1	0.97.5
Langston, Martin				1	0.37.5
Long, George	300	1000			1.50.0
Long, Isaac				1	0.37.5
Long, Maples				1	0.37.5
Love, Thos. B.	320	1500		1	2.62.5
Maxwell, James				1	0.37.5
Morris, William M.	134	200			0.30.0
Morris, William				1	0.37.5
Mattax, Rachel	79	300			0.45.0
Manes, Hirum (*)				1	0.75.0
Mitchell, William (124)	158	800		1	1.57.5
Miller, John	60	300		1	0.82.5
Morton, Silas	80	150		1	0.60.0
McClary, Robt. W.	320	1800	2 (1500)	1	5.32.5
Moreland, Joseph				1	0.37.5

Name					
Mitchel, Reace	260	500			0.75.0
Maxwell, John				1	0.37.5
Mitchell, Thos. H.	240	300		1	0.82.5
Morgan, Joshua	474	2000		1	3.37.5
Morgan, Samuel	80	100		1	0.52.5
Mcalestor, Wesley	160	300			0.45.0
McCrosky, Robert	150	700		1	1.42.5
Moore, William	180	550		1	1.20.0
Moss, Edward	160	300			0.45.0
Mashburn, David	80	200		1	0.67.5
Miller, John (125)	130	300		1	0.82.5
Newton, Edward	369	1000		1	1.87.5
Neal, Abraham B.	215	600		1	1.27.5
Pickens, Robert	160	600		1	1.27.5
Pickens, Nancy	480	2000	4 (2300)		6.45.0
Pickens, Charles A.				1	0.37.5
Patterson, Trion				1	0.37.5
Queener, John	160	1000			1.50.0
Queener, G.W.	160	400		1	0.97.5
Queener, G.C.				1	0.37.5
Randolph, Patton	120	250			0.37.5
Randolph, Jeptha				1	0.37.5
Randolph, Lancaster				1	0.37.5
Reasily/Reavly, Hugh	160	500		1	1.12.5
Shamblin, William	107	400		1	0.97.5
Snoddy, Saml.	160	200		1	0.67.5
Slaughler, Isaac				1	0.37.5
Short, John B. (126)				1	0.37.5
Short, Mary	80	400			0.60.0
Smith, Loftam N.				1	0.37.5
Seybert, John	160	500			0.75.0
ditto	160	185			0.27.75
Seybert, John Jr.				1	0.37.5
Stone, Edward			1 (700)	1	1.42.5
Smith, Collins	640	2500		1	4.12.5
Smith, Jackson	1040	5000	6 (3600)		12.90.0
ditto	185	1000			1.50.0
ditto	160	160			0.24.0
Smith, Silas	320	800		1	1.57.5
Smith, Gregory				1	0.37.5

Name					
Swafford, Richard	240	700		1	1.42.5
Swafford, Alfred				1	0.37.5
Swafford, Thos. (127)				1	0.37.5
Senter, James	319	1000		1	1.87.5
Shamblen, George	140	300		1	0.82.5
Stephenson, W.S.				1	0.37.5
Stephenson, Andrew	181	800			1.20.0
Thompson, Thos.	319	1000			1.50.0
Thompson, John	71	100			0.15.0
Vaughn, Thomas	220	925		1	1.76.25
Vinsant, Nancy (*)	112	400			1.20.0
Wallen, Isaac				1	0.37.5
Wilson, Richard	74	500			0.75.0
Watkins, Mary	80	300			0.45.0
White, William	400	1200		1	2.17.5
Whiat, Drewry	90	200			0.30.0
Wolf, Samuel			3 (1400)	1	2.47.5
Wolf, John	80	350			0.52.5
Wilson, William (128)				1	0.37.5
Whiat, Alfred				1	0.37.5
Wallen, Thomas	190	800		1	1.57.5
Wallen, Elizabeth	220	400			0.60.0
White, Moore John	230	600		1	1.27.5
Wilson, Enoch (*)				1	0.75.0

Total Taxpayers: 154, Slaves: 24, Taxes Collected: $135.93

1836 TAX LIST - DISTRICT 16 (CALHOUN)

NAME	ACRES	VALUE	SCHOOL LAND	VALUE	SLAVES 12 to 50	WP	TOTAL TAX
Atkinson, Asberry A	186	1000				1	1.87.5
Arnold, Daniel (129)			160	120			0.18.0
Amos, John						1	0.37.5
Amos, Charles						1	0.37.5.
Austin, John					3 (1300)	1	2.32.5
Black, Mark						1	0.37.5
Brock, Blanigel	248	1000				1	1.87.5
Bunch, Paul	160	800					1.35.0
Bunch, Cager						1	0.37.5
Bunch, Martin						1	0.37.5
Bunch, Joseph						1	0.37.5
Bates, William	5.35	1920	18 (1 lot)	80 (150)		1	3.60.0
Bowerman, John	360	500					0.75.0
Brittian, William	160	400				1	0.97.5
Burch, Richerson E.						1	0.37.5
Brookshire, James (130)	80	100				1	0.52.5
Bracket, Joseph						1	0.37.5
Bridges,Jas .S. & Morgan (*)			4 lots	450			1.35.0
Beavers, Major (*)			3 lots	135			0.41.0
Beavers, Spencer (*)			2 lots	125			0.37.5
Brinley, Stephen (*)	160	300					0.90.0
Castelo, Washington						1	0.37.5
Camp, John	295	1200				1	2.07.5
Cantrell, David			100	75			0.11.75
Clark, David						1	0.37.5
Camp, Thomas						1	0.37.5
Clark, Daniel						1	0.37.5
Courtney, John M.	137	500				1	1.12.5
Camp, Sterling	796	2990	40	40	1 (600)		5.44.5
Colville, George (*)	240	1500			3 (2000)		10.52.0
Caldwell (*) (131)			1 lot	30			0.09.0
Dethro, Silas						1	0.37.5
David/Davis, Alfred						1	0.37.5

Earnest, F.W.						1	0.37.5
Eddington, J.W.			2 lots	325		1	0.86.25
Elliote, John						1	0.37.5
Farringworth, Solomon	80	478	22.5	22		1	1.12.5
Faut, Solomon					1 (400)	1	0.97.5
Farmon, Jonathan						1	0.37.5
Fyffe, Isaac (*)	93	93					0.27.5
Gage, Ebenezer						1	0.37.5
Goodwinn, L.						1	0.37.5
Griffith, William	160	250				1	0.75.0
Griffith, John						1	0.37.5
Haney, Robert						1	0.37.5
Hampton, William (132)	114	200				1	0.67.5
Hambright, Peter	232	1000				1	1.87.5
Hambright, John	231	1500				1	2.62.5
Hambright, Nancy	78	500					0.75.0
Hambright, G.R.						1	0.37.5
Hambright, Benjamin					1 (500)	1	1.12.5
Hawk, Madison C.	160	600			1 (500)	1	2.02.5
Hays, John F.						1	0.37.5
Helms, J.C.						1	0.37.5
Helms, Joseph S.						1	0.37.5
Helms, Thomas						1	0.37.5
Hampton, Wade	173	350				1	0.90.0
Helms, William	100	300					0.45.0
Hickey, James			120	20			0.03.0
Helms, John	240	400					0.60.0
Gentry, James O. (133)			1 lot	400			0.40.0
Johnson, W.S.			1 lot	300		1	0.82.5
Johnson, Joel	160	400					0.60.0
Jenkins, John					1 (400)		0.60.0
Jones, William			1 lot	100			0.15.0
Jones, Reece			1 lots	300		1	0.82.5
Johnson, Lewis						1	0.37.5
Johnson, William						1	0.37.5
King, John M.						1	0.37.5
Kear, James			1 lot	160		1	0.61.5
Leomens, William	160	500					0.75.0
Long, Henry						1	0.37.5
Leo, Nicholas						1	0.37.5

Liner, Oswalt	156.75	300				1	0.82.5
Laughter, Wiley						1	0.37.5
Lock (*) (134)	160	300					0.90.0
Lavendor, George M. (*)			1 lot	50			0.15.0
McClatchy, John	880	4929	71	71	4 (1850)		10.27.5
McClatchy, A.P.	160	1000				1	1.87.5
McKamy, William	8000	3200				1	5.17.5
McDowel/McDaniel, John	136.5	500				1	1.12.5
McConnell, Joseph						1	0.37.5
Manker, Bryon						1	0.37.5
McCallie, William T.	338	2000				1	3.37.5
Morgan, Silas	100	200					0.30.0
Morgan, Richard	40	80				1	0.49.5
Morgan, Silas S.						1	0.37.5
McSpadden, James			2 lots	1250		1	2.25.0
Nicholas, Frederick	63	500				1	1.12.5
Mires, Thomas						1	0.37.5
McGuire, William (135)						1	0.37.5
McAllister, Wesley						1	0.37.5
Morgan, Gideon	495	1550					2.32.5
McGee & McCarty	1019.5	4640	21 lots	2143			10.17.5
Meadlin, Macklin (*)			1 lot	40			0.12.0
McCoy Heirs (*)	80	150					0.45.0
Night, Dennis						1	0.37.5
Owen, Daniel			1 lot	400			0.60.0
Owen, P.C.			3 lots	307		1	0.83.5
Patterson, Silas						1	0.37.5
Porter, William B.			1 lot	100			0.15.0
Pitner, Adam	109	400	1 lot	100			0.75.0
Prather, Thomas						1	0.37.5
Price, William (*)			2 lots	100			0.30.0
Rogers, Henry	180	500				1	1.12.5
Rogers, E.H. (136)						1	0.37.5
Rogers, James H.						1	0.37.5
Ross, Nathaniel						1	0.37.5
Rowls, George						1	0.37.5
Reid, G.W.						1	0.37.5
Rogers, William			1 lot	20		1	0.40.5
Rogers, John Sr.			1 lot	150		1	0.60.0

Name							
Rollings, George (*)						1	0.75.0
Ross, Lewis (*)	600	4200	75	300			13.50.0
Summers, Hamilton						1	0.37.5
Smidly/Smedly, John						1	0.37.5
Street, John						1	0.37.5
Spark, Abijah						1	0.37.5
Stanfield, James			64	100			0.15.0
Stephenson, William Sr.	216	2000				1	3.37.5
Swinford, Jonithan(137)						1	0.37.5
Shipley, Aquiller	80	150				1	0.60.0
Smith, Elitia						1	0.37.5
Simpson, Richard						1	0.37.5
Stephenson, William W. (*)			3 lots	99			0.29.5
Turk, Archibald, R.	664	3000	120, 5 lots	120, 680	2 (1000)	1	7.57.5
Teal, William						1	0.37.5
Thornbury, William						1	0.37.5
Thornbury, Lovina	80	250					0.37.5
Taylor, Levi						1	0.37.5
Turnley (*)	420	600	160	100			2.10.0
Vincent, Reuben						1	0.37.5
Varnold, Elizabeth	166	800					1.20.0
Varnold, David N.						1	0.37.5
Whitton, Archibald	80	150					0.22.5
Whitten, Jonathan (138)						1	0.37.5
Whitecotton, Bury						1	0.37.5
Wolf, Elizabeth	360	1300					1.95.0
Wolf, John						1	0.37.5
Wear, John M.C.	320	3000					4.50.0
Wallin, John						1	0.37.5
Wear, David	245	1000				1	1.87.5
Wilson, James						1	0.37.5
Woodall, Isaiah						1	0.37.5
Williams, Daniel					1 (500)	1	1.12.5
Walker, Henry						1	0.37.5
Wear, John (*)			2 lots	60			0.18.0
Westwood, John (*)			3 lots	15			0.04.5
Waterhouse, Richard (*)	160	450					1.35.0
White, John (*)	40	30					0.09.0
Wallen, Jesse (*) (139)	923	2900					8.70.0

O Kelly, Nimrod (*)   160   38   0.10.5

Total Taxpayers: 154, Slaves: 18, Taxes Collected: $177.80

1836 TAX LIST - DISTRICT 17 (COLUMBUS)

NAME	ACRES	VALUE	SCHOOL LAND	VALUE	SLAVES 12 to 50	WP	TOTAL TAX
Armstrong, A.N. (143)	190	4000				1	6.37.5
Armstrong, William			1 lot	50			0.07.5
Augusta, John	80	50					0.07.5
Baker, George Jr.						1	0.37.5
Bradford, David						1	0.37.5
Bryant, John Jr.	80	250					0.37.5
Bigham, David						1	0.37.5
Burnet, Lewis M.						1	0.37.5
Baker, George Sr.	220	350					0.52.5
Baker, Joseph	406	1200				1	2.17.5
Bradford, Michael	436	800					1.20.0
Blackwell, Sylvester	120	300				1	0.82.5
Baker, William	140	600				1	1.27.5
Biggs, William M.	160	300					0.45.0
Bryant, William						1	0.37.5
Bryant, John Sr. (144)	160	800					1.20.0
Bradford, P.A.	160	600					0.90.0
Blackwell, Peter	159	500			1 (500)		1.50.0
Bradford, Hamilton						1	0.37.5
Bradford, Henry	364	1824			7 (3100)		7.38.5
Coffey, A.M. & Bradford					1 (300)		0.45.0
Crow, Moses						1	0.37.5
Conner, Alfred B.						1	0.37.5
Carson, William A.	160	300				1	0.82.5
Cobb, George						1	0.37.5
Cobb, Robert	250	760					1.14.0
Crittendon, John	160	400					0.60.0
Crittendon, Charles						1	0.37.5

Name							
Crittendon, William						1	0.37.5
Cook, Jacob	80	500					0.75.0
Cunningham, James (145)						1	0.37.5
Chunn & Patton	1274	8000					12.0.0
Dickey, Samuel	133	800					1.20.0
Dickey, James	160	500					0.75.0
Dickey, David H.	80	300					0.45.0
David, Benjamin	160	500				1	1.12.5
Davis, Robert B.	139	320				1	0.85.5
Davis, Robert						1	0.37.5
Dennis, Allen						1	0.37.5
Dickey, Samuel H.						1	0.37.5
Edmonson, John	180	600				1	1.27.5
Fox, Abram Jr.						1	0.37.5
Fox, Abram Sr.	160	300					0.45.0
Fox, Anderson						1	0.37.5
Fox, Jacob Heirs	160	500					0.15.0
Fore, A.P. (146)			1 lot	50			0.07.5
Gorden, John	180	600					0.60.0
Gillenwaters, Elijah			3 lots	100			0.15.0
Howel, William			1 lot	5			.0.0.75
Hood, P.C.S.	359	2000				1	3.37.5
Hawkins, James	320	1000			4 (2000)	1	4.87.5
Hoard, Stanwie Heirs	800	2320	2 lots	20			3.51.0
Hashkins Dennis	80	200				1	0.67.5
Heard, Abram Heirs	900	9000					13.50.0
Haney, Harrel B.						1	0.37.5
Harris, William					1 (300)	1	0.82.5
Hambright, Frederic	320	800					1.20.0
Henderson, William C.	175	1075			1 (300)	1	2.43.75
Henderson, John C.	2	600				1	1.27.5
Henderson, Mary					1 (400)		0.60.0
Jiles, William (147)					1 (300)		0.45.0
Jackson, Woody	47.25	750	2 lots	150			1.35.0
Jackson & McConnel	813.5	4948					7.42.25
Kennedy, Samuel						1	0.37.5
Kennedy, Nancy	400	400					0.60.0
Keith, Zachariah	202	1000					1.50.0
Leomons, William	248	450					0.67.5
Larimore, George K.						1	0.37.5

Name							
Lucky, John			1 lot	60		1	0.46.5
Luck, John	160	200					0.30.0
Lea, William			3 lots	15			0.02.25
Morris, James	125	500				1	1.12.5
McConnel, Samuel	155	1500	6 lots	400		1	3.22.5
McCarmie, Stephen						1	0.37.5
McCartney, John Jr.	390	2000				1	3.37.5
Mayfield, Nancy (148)	240	1150			4 (1800)		4.42.5
Mayfield, Jesse						1	0.37.5
Meigs, Elizabeth	124	1000					1.50.0
Meigs, R.G.					1 (500)		0.75.0
Moore, Jacob	160	600					0.90.0
Maize, Caleb	160	400				1	0.97.5
Maize, John (PC)	240	1200			2 (1000)		3.37.5
Mulkey, William						1	0.37.5
McCartney, John Sr.	160	300					0.45.0
Parris, Moses					2 (1000)	1	1.87.5
Price, G.W.	640	1500					2.25.0
Poe, John	90	600					0.90.0
Pangle, James			2 lots	10			0.01.5
Pearson, Alley	160	1000	1 lot	15			1.52.25
Pearson, Jesse W.						1	0.37.5
Potter, James (149)						1	0.37.5
Potter, Jesse						1	0.37.5
Pickins, Canady						1	0.37.5
Rice, Henry	158	1000			2 (1200)		3.30.0
Ryan, Albert G.						1	0.37.5
Reid, Samuel M.			1 lot	300		1	0.82.5
Sanford/Sapford, Henry Sr.			2 lots	100			0.15.0
Shield, Banner	145	725	1 lot	15			1.11.0
Scarborough, John	331	1200				1	2.17.5
Scarborough, William	80	250				1	0.75.0
Shamblin, John	704	820				1	1.60.5
Taylor, Samuel			3 lots	200			0.30.0
Tedford, Ralph E.						1	0.37.5
Underdown, George	113	600					0.90.0
Vaughn, Mumford						1	0.37.5
Walker, William (150)						1	0.37.5
Weir, Samuel	175	1000			1 (400)	1	2.47.5

Name							
Weir, John	197	1000					1.50.0
White, John (PC)	53	530	9 lots	750	5 (2000)		5.07.0
Whitton, William						1	0.37.5
Wallen, James						1	0.37.5
Wilkerson, Lawson						1	0.37.5
Waid, Elijah						1	0.37.5
Whiat/Wheat, Drewry	90	1100				1	0.97.5
Wilson, Wm. J.B.						1	0.37.5
Wilson, Benjamin						1	0.37.5
Walker, James	160	320				1	0.85.5
Wallen, Jesse	160	200				1	0.67.5
Wilson, James	111	166					0.24.75
True, Thomas					1 (450)		0.67.5

Total Taxpayers: 123, Slaves: 35, Taxes Collected: $156.87

Index

McMinn County, Tennessee Tax Lists

1829-1832, 1836

A

ACKINSON - See ATKINSON
ACRED, John 26, 70
ACTHISON - See ATKINSON
ADAMS, Bird [1836-1]
    Burgess 169, [1836-4]
    Daniel 14, 77
    Giles 14
    John 20, 62, 160, 217, [1836-6]
    Joseph M. 210
    Joshua 7, 67
    Nelson 91
    Saml. 1, 91
    Thomas 163, 190
    William 1, 14, 82, 91, 200
    Wm. L. 150
ADKIN, ADKINS, ATKINS
    Charles 95, 222
    Leomon [1836-4]
    Wade H. 43
AGEE
    Ambrose 29, 86, 124, 208
AIKIN, AKIN, Isaac 70, 196
    John 102, 130
    Saml. J. 37, 95, 124
    Thomas (Thos.) 43, 104, 114, 173, 226, [1836-7]
AIRHART - See AYRHEART
AKIN - See AIKIN
ALASON, Joseph 148
ALBERT
    James [1836-4]
    Wm. 3, 84, 137, 196, [1836-1]
ALEXANDER, Hamilton L. 181
    John 86
    Jos. M. 43, 104, 114, 226
    Joseph [1836-15]
    J.F. [1836-8]
    Saransay 124
ALLEN
    Ananias (Nias) 17, 64, 74, 132
    Archibald B. [1836-10]
    Benjamin 22, 60, 122, 198, [1836-6]
    Cox & West [1836-3]
    Edward 5, 147, 214
    Heemery 214
    John 34, 64, 172, 194, 204, [1836-6], [1836-9]
    Jonathan 34
    Lee P. [1836-15]
    Lew 140
    Sparten 147, 214
    William 3, 34, 147, 204, [1836-10]
    Wm. B. 29, 86, 173, 181
ALLISON, William P. [1836-15]
AMARINE, George 43
    Henry 14, 77, 134, 179
    Isham 17, 74
AMOS, AMOUS
    Charles [1836-16]
    Jno. F. 144, 202
    John [1836-16]
    Wm. 20
AMOUS - See AMOS
ANDERSON
    Daniel 17, 74, 158, 186
    Isaac 47, 112, 169, 188, [1836-4]
    Jesse 43, 114

John 17, 74
Martin (Martin D.) 155, 183, [1836-5]
Saml. 17, 74, 158, 186
William [1836-4], [1836-11]
William W. (Wm. W.) 43, 104, 114, 226 (2), [1836-7]
ANGEL, ANGLE
   Hezekiah (H.K.) 34, 77, 132, 210, [1836-11]
AREHART - See AYRHEART
ARMSTED, William [1836-10]
ARMSTRONG, Abel 26
   Absolem (Absalom) 34, 64, 132, 224, [1836-12]
   Alfred 49
   Allen 34, 158, [1836-11], [1836-12]
   A.N. 108, 160, [1836-17]
   Andrew 132, 204, [1836-12]
   Baker 34 (2), 64 (2), 132, 204, [1836-12]
   Benj. D. (B.D.) 43 114
   Casey [1836-12]
   Clinton [1836-12]
   Gary A. 17, 74, 186
   Eli (Eli D., Elihu, Elihu D.) 47, 100, 169, 188, [1836-8]
   James 41, 108, [1836-12]
   Jesse 34, 64, 132
   John 17, 34 (2), 64, 74, 132, 204, [1836-12]
   Newton 217
   Robert 104
   Robert, Moses & A. 49
   Samuel (Saml.) 132, [1836-12]
   Thomas 34, 64, 132, 204, [1836-12]
   William Jr. [1836-12]
   William Sr. [1836-12]
   William (Wm.) 34 (2), 64 (2), 132 (2), 204, [1836-17]
   Wm. P. [1836-12]
ARNEL - See ARNOLD
ARNOLD, ARNEL, Allen 204

Daniel [1836-16]
Prince 49
ARNWINE
   Albartis (Albertis) 84, 137, 196, [1836-4]
   John (J.) 3, 84 (2), 111, 137, 196 (2), [1836-4]
ARTHUR
   Wm. (Wm. J.) 9, 102, 140, 215
ASH
   Hugh (Hu. B.) 5, 73, 147, 214
   James R. 73, 147, 214, [1836-15]
   Robert 5, 73, 147, 214, [1836-15]
ASKINS, Henry 122
ATCHLY
   Amos (Amos R.) 155, 190
   Seth 190
   Thomas [1836-15]
ATKINS - See ADKINS
ATKINSON, ADKINSON, ACKINSON, ACTHISON
   A.H. 173
   Asbury (Asberry A.) 37, 95, 181, [1836-16]
   Henry [1836-9]
   James 11, 60, 126, 222
   John 11, 60, 122, 140, 198, [1836-9], [1836-10]
   Jonas [1836-3]
   Wm. 3, 84, 137, 196
AUGUSTA, John [1836-17]
AUSTIN
   John 43, 104, 114, 226, [1836-16]
   Thos. 1, 91, 150
AUTREY, AUTERY, AUSRY
   Readicke [1836-8]
   Stephen 134, 179, [1836-8]
AYRES, Joseph C. 43, 104
AYRHEART, AREHART, AIRHART
   Peter 34, 64, 132, 133, 204, [1836-6]

B

BABER, Thomas 153, 155
BACKSTER - See BAXTER
BAILES, BALES, Jno. 132
    Thomas 104
BAILEY, BAILY, BALEY, BAYLEY
    Haysman (Hayman) 95, 181
    James 35, 108, [1836-12], [1836-15]
    John 41, 108, 172, 217, [1836-14]
    Levi 41
    Lewis 41, 108, 160
    Lucy (Lucey) 37, 124, 181
    Robert 212
    Sam. P. [1836-15]
    Washington [1836-15]
    Wesley (Westly) 37, 95, 134, 181
BAKER
    Alexander 43, 102, 140, [1836-3]
    Andrew 41, 108, 161, 217
    Benjamin M. 172, [1836-8]
    Chrisley 7, 67, 163, 190, [1836-11]
    Esther - Heirs 161, 217
    George 41, 108, 172, 217
    George Jr. [1836-17]
    George Sr. [1836-17]
    Henry 9
    James [1836-7], [1836-15]
    John 206, 210, [1836-6], [1836-11]
    Joseph 41, 108, 161, 217, [1836-17]
    Reubin, (Reubin J.) 130, 172, 179
    Richmond 5
    Thos. 153
    William (Wm.) 41, 108, 161, 217, [1836-17]
BALINGER, David 3
    Joseph 3
    Peter 3, 84, 138, 196
BALL
    Levin L. (L.L., Leuen L.), 11, 60, 110, 126, 222, [1836-9]
BALLARD, Fail 111
    Wm. M. 122
BALLEW, BELLEW
    Jefferson 24, 88, 155, 183, [1836-5]
    William [1836-4], [1836-5], [1836-7]
    William H. [1836-5]
    Wm. M. 24, 88, 155, 173, 183
BALYS, Pike [1836-5]
BARB
    Abraham, A. 33, 80, 153 (2), 206 (2), [1836-6]
BARCLAY
    Elihu S., (E.S)., 43, 104
BARGER, George [1836-6]
BARKER
    Burrel Jr. (Burrel) 57, 136, 192, [1836-15]
    Burrel Sr. (Burrel) 5, 57, 136, 192, [1836-15]
    James G. 49
    Thomas 41, 108
BARKSDALE, Allen [1836-14]
    Nathaniel (Nathan) 1, 91, 150, 200
    Sherrod [1836-14]
BARNES, BARNS
    Abraham 49, 166, 219
    Daniel 138, 196
    Pleasant 14, 77, 130, 210, [1836-8]
    Susanah [1836-12]
BARNETT, BARNET, BARNITT
    James 39, 41, 55, 108, 142, 160, 217, [1836-13]
    James M. 24, 88, 183, [1836-6]
    John W. 33, 80, 153, 206, [1836-6]
    Josephas .D. 43, 104, 114, 226
    Lemual 39
    Mitchell 155

Robert C. 206
Robt. [1836-11]
Samuel (Saml.) 59, [1836-11]
Saml. H. 80, 153, 206
William (Wm.) 33, 80, 153, 206, [1836-6]
Wm. H. 33, 80, 153, 206
William O. [1836-7]
BARRETT, James W. [1836-7]
BASINGER, BAYSINGER
   Jacob 64, 132, 226, [1836-11]
   Mathias 35
   Michael 64, 172, 204, [1836-15]
BASS, Wm. 1
BATES, Ezekiel 181
   James 181
   William (Wm.) 37, 95, 124, 181, [1836-16]
BATRUM - See BUTRAM
BAYSINGER - See BASINGER
BAXTER, BACKSTER
   Lee (Levi) 14, 77, 134, 179
BAYLEY - See BAILEY
BEALER - See BEELER
BEAN, BEEN, BEENE
   Jacob 29, 67, 86
   Jesse 7, 67, 163
   John 29, 86
   Richard [1836-11]
   Wm. 7, 67, 163
   Wm. Jr. 29, 86
   Wm. Sr. 29
BEASLEY, BESLEY, Joseph 91
   Josiah 1
BEAVER, BEAVERS, BEVER
   Benjamin [1836-8]
   Berry [1836-5]
   Hyram [1836-8]
   James [1836-3]
   John [1836-8] (2)
   Major [1836-16]
   Spencer (Spenser, S.) 43, 104, 114, 226, [1836-7], [1836-16]
   Wm. 134, 179

BECK, John H. [1836-2]
BECKET
   Josiah 14, 77, 130, 190
   Thos. 14, 77, 130, 210, [1836-11]
BECKHAM, BICKHAM
   Jesse 5, 57, 136
BEDFORD, Jonas 148
   Stephen 9, 102, 140, 215, [1836-8]
BEELER, BELER, BEALER
   Allen 9, 102
   John 35, 64, 132, 204, [1836-11]
   Joseph [1836-4]
   Sally 140
BEEGLES, David [1836-5]
BEEN - See BEAN
BELCHER, John [1836-4]
   Noah [1836-13]
BELK, BELT, Isaac 161, 217
BELL, BEAL, James 108
   John 3, 84, 137, 196
   Sarah 9, 102
   Wm. 20, 108, 161, 217
BELLEW - See BALLEW
BENNETT, BENNET, BENNITT
   Aron 9, 102, 140
   Matilda 22
   John C. [1836-1]
BENSON, John 188
   Mathias 226
BENTON, BINTON
   Edmund (Edmon) 39, 59, 146, 212, [1836-13]
   J.H. 112 (3), 188
   Jeremiah 146, 212
   Jesse H. 100, 169, [1836-3], [1836-13]
   John 14, 77, 134, 179
   Robert A. 212
   Thomas (Thos.) 14, 77, 134, 179, [1836-10]
BERRY & FOUT, 229
BESLEY - See BEASLEY
BESS, Henry [1836-9]

BEVER - See BEAVER
BEVINS, Nathaniel 57, 136, 192
BIBLE, Henry 24, 88, 155
BICKHAM - See BECKHAM
BIGGS
   William M. (Wm., Wm. M.) 20, 62, 144, 202, [1836-17]
BIGHAM, BINGHAM
   Andrew 49, 98, 166, 219
   Benjamin 5, 57, 136, 192
   B.R. [1836-11]
   David [1836-17]
   Eli 49, 98, 156
   Mary [1836-15]
   Matilda [1836-15]
BILER, John [1836-12]
BILLINGSLY
   E.H. [1836-8]
   James 22, 93, 148 (2), 194, [1836-8]
   Jesse 148, 194
   Joseph 22, 93, 145, 194, 208
   Walter (Walter Jr.) 22, 93, 148, 194, [1836-8]
   Walter Sr. 22, 93, 148, 194
BINGHAM - See BIGHAM
BINTON - See BENTON
BIRCH, George [1836-1]
BIRDWELL, Robert 47
BIRKS - See BURK
BISHOP, Eli 215
   Isaac 215, [1836-3]
   James 215, [1836-3]
   Joseph 215, [1836-3]
BITTEE, BITTELL
   George 102, 140, 215
BIVEM, Joseph [1836-12]
BIVEMS, Nathaniel [1836-15]
BLACK, John S. 53, 64
   Joseph [1836-11]
   Mark [1836-16]
BLACKBURN, BLACKBORN
   James 35, 37, 64, 95, 123, 173, 204, 222, [1836-6]
   Jesse 35, 64, 173, 204, [1836-11]
   John [1836-11]
   Maize [1836-11]
   Robert 35, 64, 172, 204
   Saml. 35, 64, 173, 204
BLACKHORN, James [1836-6]
BLACKSTONE - See BLAXTON
BLACKWELL, James 212
   Julius W. [1836-7]
   Peter 20, 62, 144, 202, [1836-17]
   Samuel J. [1836-9]
   Sylvester [1836-17]
BLADE, Isaac 91
BLAIR, James [1836-15]
   John 172, 205, [1836-10]
   J.L. [1836-6]
   Samuel 183
   William [1836-10]
BLAKELY, BLAKLEY
   Saml. 102, 215
BLANKENSHIP, BLANKINGSHIP
   Elijah 14, 111
   Inda [1836-8]
   Isam (Isom) 134, 179, [1836-8]
   John 43, [1836-8]
   John W. 100
   Thomas 122
BLARE, Samuel [1836-5]
BLASE, Samuel [1836-5]
BLAXTON, BLACKSTONE
   Aigil (Nigil, Argyle) 153
BLEVINS, Allen 126, 198
BLOOM, [No name given] 212
   E.P. [1836-12]
BLYTHE
   Saml. (Saml. M.) 26, 70, 119, 177, [1836-1]
BOATMAN
   John 124, 130, 210, [1836-11]
   Robert 53, 95, 124, 181
   Wm. 53, 95, 124
BOBERSON, Elihu [1836-11]
BOCK, Jeremiah 31
BODINE, James [1836-3]
BOGART
   Charles 172, 226, [1836-7]

Solomon (S.) 43, 104, 114, 204,
  226, (in F), [1836-7],
  [1836-8], [1836-10],
  [1836-12], [1836-14]
  Solomon & Co. 43, 104, 114
BOGGAS, BOGGUSS
  Abijah [1836-2], [1836-3]
BOGGS, John O. 3, 84, 138, 196
BOID - See BOYD
BOILER - See BYLER
BOLING, BOLIN, BOLDING,
  BOWLING, BOULING
  Allen 9
  Collins 53, 158, 221, [1836-14]
  James 20, 62, 144, 158, 202,
    [1836-14]
  John 20, 62, 173, 202
  Joseph 20, 62
  Obediah (Odadiah) 20, 62, 144,
    202, [1836-14]
  Samuel [1836-13]
  Sidney 17, 74
  William L. (Wm., Wm. L.) 20,
    53, 62, 173, 202, [1836-14]
BOND
  Amon (Amond) 24, 88, 155,
    183
  Benjamin (Benj.) 24, 88, 155,
    183, [1836-6] (2)
  Joannah (Joana) 155, 183,
    [1836-6]
  Joshua 24, 88, 155, 183, [1836-
    6]
  Peter 24
  Simon [1836-6]
BONNER
  Ezekiel (Erekiel)11, 60, 122,
    198, [1836-9]
  James 11, 60, 122, 198, [1836-
    9]
  Moses [1836-9]
BOOKOUT, Wright [1836-14]
BOON, Daniel 153, 206
  Israel (Izarel) 33, 80, 153, 206,
    [1836-6], [1836-12]
  Jesse 5, 35, 64, 132, 204

Jonathan 33, 64, 153, 206
Joseph 49, 98
Sarah 80, 153, 206
BORING, BORAN, BOWING
  Nicholas 39, 59, 146, 212
BOTTARN, Allen [1836-2]
BOTTOM, Allen [1836-2]
BOWEN, Joseph [1836-12]
BOWERS, BOWER
  James 114, 226
  John, John Jr., John W. Sr. 26
    (2), 70 (2), 119 (2), 177,
    [1836-2]
BOWERMAN
  John 7, 67, 163, 166, 219,
    [1836-15], [1836-16]
BOWING - See BORING
BOWMAN
  George 5 (2), 57, 136 (2), 172,
    192
  Leroy 136, 192
  Levi R. 5, 57, 136, 192
  Robert P. 5, 57, 136, 192
BOWRING, Ezekiel [1836-13]
  Nicholas [1836-13]
BOYD, BOID, Francis [1836-7]
  Henry 204
  Herbert (Herbid) 24, 88, 155,
    183, [1836-5]
  John [1836-5]
  Silas 111, 117, 208
BRACKET, Joseph [1836-16]
BRADEN, James 17, 74, 158
BRADFORD
  David 161, 217, [1836-17]
  George C. 20, 144, 202
  H. 20, 173
  Hamilton (Hambleton) 20, 62,
    144, 202, [1836-17]
  Henry 20, 62, 144 (2), 202 (2),
    [1836-17]
  Henry C. 20, 62, 144, 202
  James F. (J.F.) 43, 104, 173,
    226, [1836-7]
  Mrs. Mary 33

Michael 41, 108, 161, 217,
  [1836-17]
Patten A. (P.A.) 202, [1836-7],
  [1836-17]
Samuel 160
Thomas M. 160, 217
BRADLEY, BRADLY
  Ambrose 17, 39, 55, 74, 142,
    158, 186
  Daniel 31, 59, 82, 146 (2)
  Johnston 148
  Widow [1836-4]
  William 43, 104, 169
BRADOE, Ashael H. 7
BRADSHAW, Gannon [1836-9]
BRANDON, BRAMDON, BRANDOM
  Ann (Anne) 150, 200
  Calvin [1836-1]
BRAMELET
  Nathan 22, 93, 148, 194
BRANHAM, BRANUM, BRANNUM
  Jefferson 26, 70, 119, 177,
    [1836-2]
  John 1, 91
  Parmer 26, 70, 119, 177
  Wm. 14
BRAXLY, Widow [1836-4]
BRAZEAL, BRAZEALE, BREAZEALE,
  BREAZIAL
  David (David R.) 137, 196
  John W.M. [1836-7]
  William H. [1836-1]
BREESE, Wm. H. 114
BREWER, Joseph 142, 194
  Lewis 192, [1836-15]
  Mark P. 20, 62, 144, 202, 217
BREWSTER - See BRUISTER
BRIANT, BRYANT
  Elisha [1836-6]
  Ellsson (Ellisson, Elison,
    Ellisan) 3, 84, 137, 196,
    [1836-1]
  Benj. 137, 196
  James 219
  Jane 3, 84
  John 41, 108, 161, 172, 217

John Jr. [1836-17]
John Sr. [1836-17]
John W.P. [1836-6]
Katherine [1836-6]
Peter 31, 80, 82
Richd. A. 43, 104, 114
William (Wm.) 3, 84, 137, 196,
  [1836-8], [1836-15],
  [1836-17]
William F. [1836-1]
BRIDGES, James H. 114
  James S. 37, 95, 114, 226,
    [1836-7]
  James S. & Morgan [1836-16]
  John L. [1836-7]
BRINLEE, BRINLEY, BRIMLEE,
  BRIMLY
  Asa (Asa R.) 49, 98, 166, 219
  Stephen 49, 98, 166, [1836-16]
BRITTAIN, BRITTIN, BRITTIAN,
  BRITTAN
  [No name given] 173
  John 91, 150, 200
  Nathaniel 26, 70, 119, 177,
    [1836-2]
  William 37, 95, 124, 181,
    [1836-16]
  Wm. C. 95, 114, 210
BROCK, Blanigel [1836-16]
  Elbert [1836-13]
  Daniel H. [1836-13]
BROOK, Alexandria 215
  Blasengim 11, 60, 122, 222,
    230
  Elbert 39, 55, 142, 212
  Federick 39
  Henry 39
  Joel 7, 67, 163, 190
  John 60
  Terry 11, 126, 222, 230
BROOKS, Richard 39
BROOKSHIRE, BROOKSEAR,
  BROOKSHEAR
  James (Jas.) 163, 190, [1836-16]
  John [1836-11]

BROMFIELD - See BRUMFIELD
BROWDER
    Edmond 47, 100, 134, 169, 188, [1836-7]
    John W. [1836-8]
    Joseph (Jos.) 33, 80, 153, 206, [1836-6]
    J.W. [1836-7]
    Mathew 47, 100, 169, 188, [1836-7]
    S.E. [1836-8]
BROWHILL, BROWNHILL
    James 31, 82
BROWN
    A.B. [1836-4], [1836-7]
    Alexander 26, 70, 119, 177
    Aron 114
    Benjamin [1836-6]
    Hutson [1836-8]
    Isom 177
    James (James A.) 20, 62, 144, 202
    Jesse 88
    Jesse Jr. 24
    Joel K. 43, 104, 114, 226, [1836-7], [1836-13]
    John 3, 43, 104, 114, 138, 153, 173, 190, 196, 206, [1836-1]
    John D. 33, 80
    Jonathan 43
    Joseph 17, 39, 55, 153, 158, 186, 206, [1836-5], [1836-12]
    Joseph Jr. 74
    Joshua 7, 67, 163
    Mathew 173, 190
    Robert 114
    Mrs. Sarah 104, 114, 226
    Thomas (Thos.) 26, 70, 119, 144, 177, [1836-1]
    William (Wm.) 35, 64, 74, 153, 158 (2), 206, [1836-12]
    Wm. Sr. 17, 74, 158, 186
    Wm. Jr. 17, 186
    William A. 190

BROWNHILL - See BROWHILL
BROYLES
    Cornelius (Neeley) 47, 100, 169, [1836-8]
BRUISTER, BRUSTER
    William 137, 196
BRUMFIELD, BROMFIELD
    Medat (Medy, Medad) 14, 77, 130, 210, [1836-10]
BRUSTER - See BRUISTER
BRYANT - See BRIANT
BUCKNER, Burrer 9
    Garret (Garot) 153, 212
    George 80
BULLARD, Henry 37, 95, 126
    James 198
    Joseph 37, 95, 126
BUNCH, Cager [1836-16]
    Charles [1836-14]
    Joseph [1836-16]
    Martin [1836-16]
    Paul [1836-16]
BURCH, George 84
    Henry 84, 138, 196, [1836-4]
    Jno. 150
    Richerson E. [1836-16]
    Thos. 3, 84
BURGEN, Adam [1836-12]
BURGER, BERGER, Adam 224
    George 31, 82, 128, 224
    Henry 183
BURK, BURKS, BIRKS
    Allen 148, 194
    Andrew 14, 77, 130, [1836-11]
    Andrew Sr. 210
    Epha 219
    James 7, 14, 67, 163, 219
    John, John Jr., John S., 7 (2), 67 (2), 163 (2), 190, 219, [1836-11], [1836-15]
    Jonas M. [1836-15]
    Wm. 14, 77, 130, 194, 210, [1836-11]
    Willis 22, 93, 148
BURNETT, BURNET
    Edward G. 181

John 3, 70, 111, 119, 177,
   [1836-1]
John C.
John S. 181
Joseph 3, 84, 137
Joseph M. [1836-1]
Lewis 179
Lewis M. [1836-17]
Roland 3, 84, 137, 196, [1836-1]
BURNS, BURNES, BURN
   Adam [1836-5]
   John 109, 150, 200, [1836-12]
   Sherade (Shederick) 17, 74, 158
   Susanah [1836-12]
   William [1836-2], [1836-4]
BURRIS, William 188
BURTON
   Thos. 29, 86, 117, 208
BUSH
   George 104, 114, 226, [1836-7]
BUTLER, Allen 140, 215
   Andrew
BUTNER, Christian 39
BUTRAM, BUTRAME, BATRUM
   Elijah 70
   Hial [1836-2]
   Jacob [1836-2]
   James [1836-2]
   Larkin [1836-4]
   Noah [1836-2]
   Wm. 26
BUTRANAM, Allen [1836-3]
BYLER, BYLAR, BOILER
   David 17, 35, 64, 74, 132, 186
   John 17, 35, 64, 74, 186

C

CADDELL, Parson [1836-15]
CADWELL, Parson 37
CAIN, CAINS, KAIN, KEAN
   Isaac [1836-9]
   John [1836-8]
   Robert [1836-9]
   Solomon 44, 105 115, 215
   William [1836-9] (2)
   W.D. [1836-4]
CALAHAN, CALLAMAN
   James A. 11, 110, 126, 222
CALDWELL, COLDWELL
   [no name] [1836-16]
   Andrew [1836-12]
   Hance A. 62
   Robert R. 117, 208
   Robt. B. [1836-11]
   Solomon (Solomon M.) 7, 67, 163, 190
   Thomas [1836-10]
   Wm. 67, 163
   Wm. B. [1836-11]
CALHOUN, CALHOON
   James 39, 55, 142, 221, 229, [1836-14]
   William (Wm.) 142, [1836-14]
CALOWAY, John 43
   William S. [1836-4]
CAMARON, CAMERON, CAMRON
   Archibald 20, 62, 142, 144, 202, [1836-14]
   William [1836-14]
CAMEL - See CAMPBELL
CAMP
   John 9, 49, 95, 102, 124, 208, [1836-16]
   Sterling 49, 88, 166, 219, [1836-16]
   Thomas [1836-16]
   Wm. (Wm. H.) 166
CAMPBELL, CAMEL
   Andrew 35, 64, 132
   James 9, 102
   John 31, 82, 128, 142, 148, 194, 224
   Katherine [1836-13]
   Phebe (Phadro) 7, 67, 163, 230, [1836-15]
   Thomas J. 43, 104
   Victor M. [1836-7]
   Wesley 194
   Wm. 14, 77, 148, 194

CANNON
    Mary 119, 177, [1836-1]
    Wm. 26, 70
CANORD - See KINNARD
CANSLER, CANSELOR, CANSELER
    John 35, 84, 132, 204, [1836-6]
    Mary 128, 224
    Nathanl. H. 31, 43, 58, 104
    Wm. 5, 57, 128, 135, 230
CANTRELL, CANTILE
    David (D.) 17 (2), 74 (2), 158, 186 (2), [1836-12], [1836-16]
    Elijah 17, 74, 158, 186, [1836-12]
    Gabriel (G.) 17, 73, 74, 158 (2), 186, [1836-12], [1836-14]
    Isaac 17, 74, 158, 186, [1836-12]
    Jacob 17, 74, 158, 186, [1836-12]
    Jas. 144
    John M. [1836-12]
    Moses 221
    Nimrod 148, 194, [1836-8]
    Wm. [1836-12]
CARAGAN, Marcus [1836-14]
CAREYS, [No name given] 105
CARLOCK
    Isaac 17, 74, 158, 173, 186, [1836-12], [1836-14]
    Jas. C. [1836-12]
CARMACK, Joseph 198
CARNES
    John 22, 93, 148, [1836-10]
    Nicholas 41
CARNETT - See CORNETT
CARNEY, Joshua [1836-13]
    George [1836-13]
    Madison [1836-13]
CAROUTH, Walley [1836-12]
CARPENTER, CARPENNER
    Saml. 14, 102, 222
CARRELL - See CARROLL
CARRINGTON
    James 70, 119, 177, [1836-2]

CARROLL, CARREL, CARRELL
    Elijah 7, 67, 163, 181
    Henry 26, 70, 119, 177, [1836-2]
    Luke [1836-2]
    Richmond 60, 122, 198
    Samuel 122
CARROUTH
    Walter 31, 82, 128, 224
CARSON, [No name given] 44
    John 39, 55, 142
    Nancy 39, 55
    Newton 43, 104, 114
    William A. [1836-17]
CARTER
    Amos [1836-13]
    Benjamin [1836-13]
    Charles 33, 80, 153, 206, [1836-5], [1836-6]
    Edmund [1836-6]
    Erasmus (Arasmus) 183, [1836-6]
    Frederick [1836-13]
    H. 24
    Leroy [1836-1]
    Josiah 33, 80, 153, 206
    Randolph 104, 114, 226, [1836-7]
    Robert [1836-13]
    Samuel 206
    Thomas [1836-13]
    Wm. 33, 80, 153, 206
CARTWRIGHT, CARTRIGHT, CARTRITE
    John [1836-6]
    Lemual 33, 153
    Levi 33, 132, 204
    Thos. 33
CARY, Nathaniel 43
    Wm. H. & Robert M. 43
CASADA, CASIDA, CASSIDAY
    David [1836-7]
    James [1836-11]
    John (John C.) 130, 226, [1836-7]

Martin 14, 35, 64, 105, 132, 204, [1836-11]
Martin Jr. 114, 226
Reuben (Reubon) 14, 104, 114, 226, [1836-7]
William [1836-11]
CASEY, CAISEY, KASEY
   Abner 26, 70, 119
   Ambler 26, 70, 119, 177, [1836-3]
   Dempsey 88, 183
   James 164
   John [1836-3], [1836-8]
   Moses 177, [1836-3]
CASH
   Howard [1836-15]
   Thomas 93, 148, 194, [1836-8]
   Frontispiece (2)
CASIDA - See CASADA
CASKEY, John 74, 158, 212
   Thomas 55, 158, 186
CASS, CAST
   Benjamin [1836-13]
   John 212, [1836-13]
   James 59, 146, [1836-13]
   Moses (Moses H.) 212, [1836-13]
CASSIDAY - See CASADA
CASTEEL, CASTELL
   Alexander 14, 77, 130, [1836-8]
   Barney 146, 212, [1836-13]
   Edward 31, 59, 82, 128
   Elijah 14, 77, 130, 210
CASTELLO, CASTELO, CASLOW, CASTALOW
   George W. (G.W.) 37, 98, 166, 219
   Washington [1836-16]
CATE, CATES, Amos 1, 91, 150
   Charles 47, 100, 134, 179, [1836-8]
   Elijah 1, 91, 150, 200, [1836-4]
   Ephraim 29, 86, 117, 208
   George W. (G.W.) 134, 179
   Gibson 14, 200

   Gideon 35, 64, 132, 204, [1836-12]
   James 1, [1836-8]
   John 1
   Jno. B. 151, 200
   John E. 47, 100, 169, 188, [1836-8]
   Joseph 29, 117, 179
   Lucey 1, 91, 150, 200
   Robert 47, 100, 230
   Saml. 95, 151
   Simeon 47, 100, 169, 188, [1836-7]
   Thomas (Thomas Sr.) 1, 91, 151, 200, [1836-4]
   Thomas Jr. 151
   William (Wm.) 9, 14, 47, 77, 134, 173, [1836-4]
   Wm. Jr. 134, 179, [1836-8]
   Wm. Sr. 100, 179, [1836-8]
CAUES, William [1836-12]
CAVALER, Wiley 9
CAVE, William [1836-12]
CAWOOD, CAYWOOD
   Joshua B. 3, 84, 138, 196
CECIL, Thos. 3, 84, 138, 196
CELEY, Richard 31
CENTER, CENTERS -See SENTER
CERTAIN, John 20
CHAMBERS, Edmond 31, 82
   John 140
   McConnell 134, 179
CHAPMAN, CHATMAN
   Edmon (Edmon W, Edward W, Edward, E.W.) 31, 57, 75, 136, 186, 192, [1836-12]
   Lemuel [1836-6]
   Saml. 128, 224
   Willeford [1836-11]
   Wilson 31,186
CHARLES, McConnall [1836-10]
CHATMAN - See CHAPMAN
CHELTON - See SHELTON
CHESNUT
   James 17, 73, 75, 158, 186, [1836-12]

Raleigh 17, 74, 158, 186,
   [1836-12]
CHILDERS, CHILDRES, CHILDRERS
   Isaac 60, 122, 181
   John 55
   Joseph 39
   Josiah 39
   Robert 41, 108, 161, 217
   Saml. 39, 55, 142
   Walter 41, 108, 161, 217
   Wm. 30, 55, 142
CHILTON, Thomas 31, 80
CHITWOOD
   Lazarus (Lascrous, Lazeraus) 7, 53, 67, 163, 190, [1836-11]
   Pleasant 190
CHRISTIAN, CHRISTEN
   James 26, [1836-2]
   Jesse [1836-5]
   John 88, 153, 206, [1836-4]
   Lewis 24, 88, 155, 183, [1836-5]
   Wm. 24, 88, 155
CHUNN and DALTON, 20
CHUNN and PATTON, 62, 144, 202, [1836-17]
CHURCHMELL
   George W. [1836-2]
CINNARD - See KINNARD
CITZE - See SITZE
CLARK, CLARKE
   Alfred L. [1836-12]
   Benjn. 122, 198
   Daniel [1836-16]
   David [1836-16]
   John (John F., John L) 41, 108, 161, 192, 217
   Jesse [1836-2]
   William [1836-7]
CLAYTON, Henry 41
   John 49, 98, 166, 219
CLEAGE, CLIUGE, CLIAGE, CLIAGO
   Alexander 44, 104, 114, 226, [1836-7]
   David 44, 105, 114, 226, [1836-7]

Samuel (Saml.) 47, 100, 169, 226, [1836-3], [1836-4]
CLEMER, Turner 151
CLIAGEO - See CLEAGE
CLIUGE - See CLEAGE
CLOUD, George W. [1836-2]
   John 31, 82, 128
   James [1836-2]
   Osage [1836-13]
CLOWER, James 119, 177
COAT, COATES, COATS
   Abia 5, 136
   Jesse 5, 57, 136
   John [1836-3]
   Miles 5, 57, 136
   William (Wm.) 140, 215, [1836-3]
COBB, COBBS
   David A. (Davis A.) 39, 55, 142, 221 (2), [1836-13], [1836-14]
   George 217, [1836-17]
   John 17, 20, 73, 147, 214 (2), [1836-14]
   Joseph Sr. 20, 73, 147, 214
   Joseph Jr. (Joseph) 20, 73, 147, 214, [1836-14], [1836-15]
   Robert 41, 108, 161, 217, [1836-17]
COBLE, Davis A. [1836-14]
   Joseph [1836-14], [1836-15]
   John [1836-14]
COCHRAN, COCKRAM, COTCHRAN
   John 11, 60, 95, 126, 222
COCKBOAN, John [1836-13]
COCKE, John 204
COCKHORN, John [1836-13]
COE, Wesley (Westly) 120, 138
COFFEY, COFFEE
   Asbury M. (A.M.) 43, 64, 132, 204, [1836-7], [1836-17]
   Bradford [1836-17]
   Eli 35, 64, 132, 204
   James [1836-3]
   Marvell (Marvil, Mavill) 33, 64, 153, 206, [1836-6]

COFFMAN, James [1836-8]
COLDWELL - See CALDWELL
COLE, James [1836-1]
COLEY
    James 43, 104, 114, 226
COLIER
    Bannister [1836-11]
    James 5, 17, 57, 74, 136, 192, [1836-11]
    Thomas [1836-8]
    Wilson [1836-5]
COLLINS, George [1836-4]
    Henry, 91
    James 142, 144
    John 39, 55, 142
    Joseph 22, 93
    Margret 1, 91, 151
    Robert [1836-9]
    Thomas 93, 148, 194
COLTER, James 104
COLVILLE, COLVILLS
    George 37, 95, [1836-16]
    George Jr. 37, 95, 126, 222
    George Sr. 37, 95, 124, 222
    Joseph 37, 95, 126
    Mrs. Natty 114
    Robert 77
    Saml. 43, 104
    Young - Heirs (Widow & Heirs) 43, 104, [1836-7]
COMBS, Auborn [1836-10]
    Elizabeth 117, 208, [1836-10]
    Pleasant 114
    Samuel [1836-11]
    Thos. 130, 210
    Wm. 14, 77, 130, 210
CONNER, Alfred B. [1836-17]
    John [1836-15]
    Saml. 29
COOK, COOKE
    Abraham [1836-8]
    George 104, 114
    Hesekiah (Hezekiah C.) 142, 212, [1836-14]
    Jacob 49, 98, 166, 219, [1836-17]
    Jadia (Judiah) 100, [1836-3]
    John 3, 177
    John Jr. [1836-1]
    Robert F. 44
    Washing. [1836-14]
    Wm. 35, 64, 132, 204
    William H. (Wm. H.) 39 (2), 43, 59 (2), 104, 142, 212 (2), [1836-7], [1836-13]
COOPER
    Bennet 31, 64, 132, 204, [1836-6]
    E. 43, 104
    Ebenezer 173, [1836-7]
    Henry 31, 82, 128, 224
    Henry Est. [1836-14]
    James [1836-6]
    John P. (Jno. P.) 142, [1836-14]
    Philip 31, 82, 128, 224, [1836-6]
    Thomas 128, 224, [1836-6]
COOSS, Jacob [1836-13]
COPELAND
    Alexander 35, 39, 64, 172, 186, [1836-12]
    John 1, 35, 64, 172, 186, [1836-12]
    Joseph 1, 31, 91, 128, 224, [1836-12]
    Wm. 1, 91, 151
COPPACK, Aaron [1836-2]
CORN, CORNE
    George 41, 67, 163, 217
CORNETT, CARNETT, CURNETT
    James 1, 53
COTCHRAN - See COCHRAN
COUCH
    Jonathan 29, 86, 117, 208, [1836-10]
    Sylvanis 181
COURTNEY
    John (John M.) 37, 95, 126, 222, [1836-16]
COVINGTON, COVENTON
    [No name given] 77
    Wm. 22, 130, 210

COWAN, COWEN
  Andrew 14, 77, 130, 210, [1836-11]
  Campbell G. 35, 64
  David 29, 117, 208
  James E. (James C.) 37, 181
  James Jr. .29, 86, 117, 208, [1836-10]
  James Sr. 29, 86, 117, 208, [1836-10]
  Robert (P.) 35, 64, (2), 111, 132 (2)
  Rosannah 35, 64, 132, 204
  Wm. 37
COX, Benj. 29, 86, 173, 222
  G. 11, 86
  Gale [1836-12]
  George R. 14, 109, 130, 210
  G.W. 86
  Harwick 147
  James 17, 74, 158, 186, [1836-12]
  John 20, 73, 147, 214, [1836-12], [1836-15]
  Philip 29, 86
  Sarah 181
  Solomon 140
  Thomas S.A. 122, 198
  Wm. 29, 86, 117, 181
COXEY, COXY
  Absolum (Absalem, Absalom) 22, 93, 148, 194, [1836-8], [1836-9]
  George 22, 93, 148, 194, [1836-9]
  John 148, 194
CRABTREE, Thomas [1836-15]
CRAIG, Allen [1836-11]
  James 11
CRAIGHEAD, Thos. C.A. 117
CRANE, Henry 14
  William 192
CRAWFORD & MURRELL, 43, 226
CRAWFORD
  Andrew 26, 70, 119 (2), 177, [1836-2]
  James 151, 200
  John 43, 104, 114, 226
  Frontispiece (3)
  John [1836-4], [1836-7], [1836-13]
  John D. 43, 104, 204
  Jonathan 49
  Mathias 98, 166, 219
  Norman, 43, 104, 114
  Thomas 20, 142
CREW, Katherine [1836-2]
CRICKET, James [1836-6]
CRISMAN, CHRISMAN
  George C. 120
  Isaac [1836-2]
  Neeley (Nealy) 47, 100, 169, 188, [1836-4]
CRISP, James [1836-1]
CRITENDON, CRITTENDON, CRITTENDAN, CRITTINGDON, CRITTINGTON
  Charles 14, 41, 77, 108, 130, 161, 217, [1836-17]
  John 43, 161, 217, [1836-15], [1836-17]
  Nathaniel 14, 77, 130, 190, [1836-11]
  William (Wm.) 41, 108, 130, 217, [1836-17]
CROCKETT, David E. 224
  David [1836-6]
  James 128, 224
  John 82, 128, 224, [1836-12]
  John A. [1836-12]
CROELL, Israel 132
CROMWELL
  Isaac (Isaac G.) 41, 108, 161, 202, 217
  James 108, 161
  Pamas S. 41
CROW
  Benjamin S. 26, 70, 119
  Denson [1836-10]

Isaac 43, 104, 114, 226, [1836-7]
Moses [1836-17]
Robert (Robt. C.) 26, 70, 119, 177
Wm. 119, 177
Wilson 177, [1836-2]
CROWNOVER
  Benjamin (Benj.) 22, 93, 148, 194, [1836-10]
CRUIZE, CRUISE, CREWZE, CREWS
  Gilbert 47, 100, 112, 169, 188, [1836-3]
CRUMP, John [1836-11]
CRUTCHFIELD
  [No name given] 44
  Thomas (Thos.) 47, 104, 114, 226, [1836-7]
CRY, James 204
  Jonathan 204, [1836-11]
CULPEPER, CULPEPPER, CULPEPIER
  Burrel (Burrell, Burrel S.) 161, 202, [1836-14]
  Joel 41, 108, 161
  John 217
CULTON, Hugh W. 188, [1836-3]
  James 44, 47, 88, 169, 188, [1836-3]
CULWELL, Joseph [1836-11]
CUMMONS, John 224
CUNNINGHAM, CUNINGHAM
  Ebenezer 181
  Evaline [1836-6]
  James 202, [1836-17]
  John 24, 88, 155, 183, [1836-5]
  M. 183
  Marshall W. (M.W.) 88 (2), 183, [1836-7]
  Margaret 24, 88, 153
  Moses 64, 132, 183, [1836-6]
  Pleasant (P.T.) 88, 155, 183
  Saml. (Saml. B.) 126, 208, [1836-10]
  Whitfield 44
  William (Wm.) 114, [1836-7]

Wm. H. 24, 88, 155, 183, [1836-5]
Wm. H. Jr. [1836-5]
CURNETT - See CORNETT

D

DAIDSON, John D.A. [1836-7]
DALLERSON, Joseph 22
DALTON, David 44, 105, 114
DAUGER, Henry 39, 55
DANIEL, DANIELS, Amey 198
  Coleman 140, 215, [1836-8]
  Wm. 166
DARTER
  John 26, 70, 120, 177, [1836-2]
DAUGHORTY - See DOHERTY
DAUGHTY - See DOHERTY
DAVID, Alfred [1836-16]
  Benjamin [1836-17]
DAVIDSON - See DAVISON
DAVIS, [No name given] 151
  Anthony 132, 226, [1836-8]
  Aaron (Aron) 84, 139, 196, [1836-1]
  Alfred [1836-16]
  Benjamin 11, 41, 60, 108, 122, 161, 217
  Brittian [1836-4]
  Burtin 41
  Calvin 35, 65
  Elie [1836-3]
  Henry 17
  Isaac 5, 57, 136, 192, [1836-15]
  Isaiah 210
  Isarah [1836-11]
  John [1836-1], [1836-11] (2)
  Jacob 11, 60, 122
  Lewis [1836-1]
  Mathew [1836-7]
  Paul 67
  Robert 41, 108, 161, 217, [1836-17]
  Robert B. 108, 161, 217, [1836-17]

Silas 3, 84
Thomas 14
Wm. 14 (2), 77 (2), 130, 210
Wm. Estate of 226
Wm. R. 100, 169, 188
DAVISON, DAVIDSON
   James 166, 219
   Jesse 140
   Richard 166, 219
DAY, James [1836-1]
   John 120, 177
DEADRICK, DEDRICK, DEDERICK, DEADRICH
   William H. (Wm. H.) 5, 57, 136, 19, [1836-7]
DEAN, Thomas [1836-1]
DEARICK - See DERRICK
DEARMAN, DEARMAND, DEARMOND
   Allen 37
   Ellisson 222
   James 14, 44, 77, 105, 130, 230
   John 31, 59, 65, 82, 128, 173, 204, 224, [1836-13]
   John A. 95, 126, 222
   Jonas 14, 44, 105, 130
   Wm. M. (Wm.) 95, 126
DEARRING, Alfred 37, 95
DECKARD, DECKERT, DICKARD
   John 25, 47, 100, 140, 215, [1836-8]
DECKER
   Allen (Allen R.) 57, 135
DEDERICK - See DEADRICK
DEDRICK - See DEADRICK
DEHART
   John Jun. (John) 70, 120, 177
   John Sr. 70, 120
DENNIS
   Allen 22, 93, 102, 140, 148, 179, 215, [1836-8], [1836-17]
   Allen (fitin) 22
   Isham (Isom) 9, 102, 140, 215, [1836-3]

James 9, 102, 140, 215, [1836-3]
Jonathan M. 188
DENTON, Isaac 39
   James 44, 105
DERRICK, DERICK, DEARICK
   Jacob (Jacob L.) 31, 82, 128, 224, [1836-12]
   John 31, 82, 128, 224, [1836-12]
   Jonathan 100, 169, [1836-4]
   Michael (Michel, Michael C.) 31, 128 (2), 212, 224, [1836-12], [1836-13]
   Wm. E. 24
   William H. [1836-11]
DETHRO, Silas [1836-16]
DEVINE, DIVINE
   James 17, 75, 158, 186
   John 17, 75, 158, 186, [1836-14]
   Thomas Jr. 17
   Thomas Sr. 17, 75, 158, 186
DICKERSON, DICKISON, DOCKESON
   Charles [1836-10]
   Garland (Garlant) 49, 98, 166
   Griffith 49, 98, 166, 219
   John 102, 140, 215
   Thomas I. [1836-3]
DICKARD - See DECKARD
DICKEY
   David H. 41, 108, 161, 217, [1836-17]
   James [1836-17]
   James M. 217
   John F. 20, 73, 147
   John P. [1836-14]
   Samuel (Saml.) 41, 108, 161, 217, [1836-17]
   Samuel H. (Saml. H.) 41, 161, 217, [1836-17]
DICKINSON, John [1836-8]
DICKISON - See DICKERSON
DILDA, Charles [1836-13]
DILDAY, Elias [1836-6]
   Simeon [1836-13]

DILLARD, James 22
DITMORE, DITEMORE
   Edward (Edmon) 212, 224
   Eliza 146
   John 39, 59, [1836-13]
   Vincent [1836-13]
DIVINE - See DEVINE
DIXON, Edom 166, 219
   Elias 183
   Elie [1836-6]
   James 80, 153, 206
   John 9, 44, 65, 105, 114, 204
   John G. [1836-7]
   Saml. H. 155
   Samuel W. (Saml. W.) 33, 88, 153, 183, 206, [1836-6]
   Solomon 1, 91, 155
   Thomas 26, 70, 120, 177
DOAN, DONE, Ira 192, [1836-15]
   John [1836-15]
   Polly 57, 136
DOBKINS, Jesse 91, 138, 200
DOBS, Hezekiah [1836-5]
   Hiram [1836-5]
DOCKESON - See DICKERSON
DODD, Charles 196
   John [1836-4], [1836-14]
   Richard 49, 112, 166, 219
   Wm. 138, 196
DODSON, DOTSON
   Allen [1836-2]
   Archibald 26
   Doctor F. [1836-1]
   Elisha 29, 86, 117, 208, [1836-10]
   Fanny (Frances) 82, 128, 224, [1836-6]
   Henry [1836-8]
   James 39, 59, 172, 212, [1836-13]
   Jane 128
   Jesse 7, 14, 29, 86, 117 (2), 208, [1836-10] (2), [1836-11]
   Jesse Jr. 29, 86, 118, 208
   Jesse Sr. 29, 86, 208
   Jesse J. 67, 163, 190
   John 26, 67, 70, 120, 163, 177, [1836-2], [1836-13]
   Levie [1836-11]
   Nicholas P (Nicholas, Neles) 29, 93, 148, 194, [1836-11]
   Nimrod [1836-10]
   Oliver 35 65, 132, 204, [1836-7]
   Warren 93, 208, [1836-8]
   William (Wm.) 26 (2), 29, 31, 70 (2), 82, 86, 118, 120, 128, 177 (2), 224, [1836-1], [1836-2], [1836-6], [1836-8]
   William E. [1836-7]
   Wm. Jr. 208
   Wm. Sr. 118, 208
   Wm. A.D. for D. 31
DOHERTY, DAUGHTY, DORTHERLY, DAUGHORTY
   Charles 31, 59, 82, 146, 212, [1836-13]
   John [1836-15]
   Mathew 31, 59, 82, [1836-13]
   Sampson 105
DONAHOE, Irvin (Ervin) 7, 67
DONE - See DOAN
DORIAN, DORIN, DOREN, DREAN
   Charles H. 37, 95, 124, 181
   John G. 44, 105, 114, [1836-7]
DORSEY, DOSSEE
   Demmon Jr. 132, 204
   Demmon Sr. 132, 204
   Dimmon (Dimon) [1836-7], [1836-12]
   John (Jno.) 132, 204, [1836-7]
DORTHERLY - See DOHERTY
DOTSON - See DODSON
DOUGLAS, DOUGLASS, DUGLASS
   Ira 214
   James 17, 73, 147, 186, [1836-14]
   Jesse 17, 73, 147, 214
   John 111, 142, 221, [1836-14]
   Wm. 24, 88, 155, 183

William R. [1836-11]
DOUGHET, DOUTHART, DOUTHARD
   Jno. 142
   Saml. 128, 226
DRAKE, Siles [1836-15]
   Tyler 20, 62, 172, 217
DREAN - See DORIAN
DUCK
   Thomas 204
DUCKWORTH, John [1836-12]
   Saml. [1836-12]
DUGAN, DUGANE, George 206
   Thomas [1836-10]
   William (Wm.) 153, 206, [1836-12]
DUGLASS - See DOUGLASS
DUNCAN, Hiram 31
DUNEVAN, (DONEVAN?)
   Michael 41
DUNN, John 186
   Joseph 47
DUTHRO, Jacob [1836-15]
DUVESE ?, DEVISE ?
   Jacob 14, 77
DYER, Archd. 67, 163, 192
   James 26, 70, 120, 177, [1836-2]
   Joel H. 20, 62
   Thomas H. [1836-2]
   William [1836-2]

E

EADENS, EDENS
   Archd. (Archibald) 37, 95, 126, 181, [1836-10]
EARLES, ERLES
   James 44, 105, 114, 226, [1836-7]
EARNEST, F.W. [1836-16]
EASON, Randolph 114, 229
EASTERS, Solomon [1836-11]
EATON, Clem. [1836-11]
EDENS - See EADENS
EDGAR, George D. 181

   John M. 17, 75, 158
EDGEMON, Saml. 177
EDGING, EDGEING
   Joab 91, 151
   John (Johnson) 84, 200
EDINGTON, EDDINGTON
   Hubert 166
   Jesse (Jessee W., J.W.) 49, 95, 124, 181, [1836-16]
EDMISSON, EDMISTON, EDMONSON, EDMINSON, EDMONDSON
   Abraham 5, 57, 136, 192
   Amanuel 18, 73, 75
   John 41, 161, 217, [1836-17]
   Saml. 49, 98, 108, 166, 219
   Suddurth (Sudderath) 5, 153, 206
EDWARD, E,C, [1836-7]
EDWARDS Walter, 24, 88
ELDER
   James 82, 128, 215, 221
   John 93, 122
   John M. 60, 198
   John S. 148, 194, [1836-8]
   Saml. 33, 80, 153, 206
ELLEDGE, Jacob [1836-4]
   Rolan 91
ELLER, James F. [1836-13]
   Joshua [1836-13]
ELLIOT, ELLIOTT, ELLIOTE
   Jesse 31, 33, 82, 128, 224, [1836-6]
   John 31, 49, 59, [1836-13], [1836-15], [1836-16]
   J.M. [1836-6]
   Thomas 146
ELLIS
   Ezekiel 15, 77, 130, 210
   Henry 17, 55, 142, 221
   James 31
   John 39, 47, 55, 100, 142, 169, 188, 221, [1836-8]
   John J. 221, [1836-14]
   Joseph 93

Joshua 31, 82, 146, 230, [1836-6]
Josiah 212
Wm. 3, 84, 138, 196, [1836-1]
ELLISON, ELLISSON, ELLIZON
　Benjamin [1836-4]
　Hinson 3, 84, 138, 196, [1836-2], [1836-4]
　James 26
　Robert (Robert Sr.) 26, 70, 120, 138, 196
　William 190
EMERSON, EMMERSON
　Allen [1836-5]
　William (Wm.) 7, 67, 163, 190, [1836-11]
ENGLAND
　Joseph 44, 105, 114, 226, [1836-7]
ENSLY, INSLEY
　Robert (R.) 35, 57
　Wm. 35, 204
EPPERSON, EPISON
　Benjamin 15, 17
　Jesse (Jessee Sr.) 15, 77, 134, 179
　Jesse Jr. 134, 208
　Joseph 15, 194
　Peter 7, 67
　Thomas 15, 77, 134, 179
ERIXON, John [1836-8]
ERLES - See EARLES
ERSKINE, ERSKIN
　Hugh 186, [1836-8]
ERWIN, IRWIN, IRVIN
　Benjamin 31, 82, 128, 224
　James (Jas. Jr.) 111, 126, 222, [1836-9]
　John 60, 126, 222, [1836-9]
　Wm. 11, 60, 126, 222
ESSMAN, ESMON
　John 18, 75, 158, [1836-13]
ESSPERSON, John [1836-8]
ETTER, Peter 33, 80, 153, 206
EUBANKS, Catharine 138
　George 3, 84, 155

Philip 24, 84
EVANS, EAVANS, J. 102
　James 102, 186
　John S. 186
EVERET, Jeremiah 5
　John 5
EVERTON, EVVERTON
　[no name] 18, 75, 158, 221
　Thomas [1836-14]
EWING, EWIN, Jonathan 9
　Saml. (Saml. A.) 35, 65, 133, 204

F

FAGAN. Jno. 159, 186
FAIN
　Ebenezer 24, 80, 155, 183, [1836-6]
FAIR, Thomas [1836-5]
FANN, Caleb [1836-12]
　Malcath [1836-12]
FAUT, Solomon [1836-16]
FARLESS, FAIRLESS
　James (Jas. Sr.) 22, 102, 135, 148
FARMER, Edward 26
　Henry 57, 136
　James [1836-14]
　Jesse 5, 57, 136
　John K. 44, 105, 115, 225, [1836-7]
　John W. 44, 105, 115, 227
　Robert (Robert A.) 57, 111, 155
　Wm. 5, 24, 57, 88, 136, 155, 192
FARMON, Jonathan [1836-16]
FARNSWORTH, FARNESWORTH, FARRINGWORTH
　Solomon 37, 95, 124, 181, [1836-16]
FARRIS, PHARRIS, PHARRISS
　Jeremiah 60, 123, 198, [1836-9]
　John 12, 60, 122, 196

Stephen (Stephen Sr.) 12, 122, 198, [1836-9]
FAULKNER, R. [1836-4]
FELKER
    Peter 31, 33, 80, 128, 153, 207, 224, [1836-6]
FENNEEL, J.B. [1836-12]
FETZOOR, Isaac 214
FERGUSON, Wm. [1836-12]
FIELDS, FIELD
    Beeson 26, 70, 120, 177, [1836-2]
    David 9
    Green [1836-2]
    John 177, [1836-2]
    Joseph 26, 70, 120, 177
    Thomas 70, 120, 177, [1836-1], [1836-2]
FIRESTONE, Alfred 161, [1836-12]
    Anthony 186
    Daniel 186
    David 158, 186
    D.S. [1836-12]
    Matthias (Mathias) 18, 75, 159, 186, [1836-12]
    Samuel 18, 75, 159, 186, [1836-12], [1836-14]
    Simpson 186
    Wm. 18, 75, 158, 186, [1836-12]
FISHER, Augustus [1836-7]
    Jacob [1836-7]
    John. B. 109, 135, [1836-10]
FITCH, Isaac [1836-1]
    Jacob 3, 84, 196, [1836-1]
FITE
    Elias (Eli) 35, 65, 133, 205, [1836-12]
    Henry 35, 65, 133, 205, [1836-12]
    Peter (Peter Jr.) 35, 65, 133, 230, [1836-12]
    Peter Sr. 35, 65, 133, 205, [1836-12]

FITZGERALD, FITSGERALD, FITSJERALD, FITZGARREL, FITZJARREL
    Daniel [1836-9]
    Jesse 213
    John 7, 210
    Joseph (Joseph B.) 3, 84, 138, 196, [1836-1]
    Martin 122
    Saml. 11, 123
FITZPATRICK, Joel 169
FJARRIL, Archibald [1836-9]
    Asa [1836-9]
FLANIGAN, FLANAGAN, FLANAGIN, FLANIGIN, FLENNIKIN
    James 9, 102, 140, 215, [1836-8]
    John 9, 22, 102, 140, 215
FOGGY, James [1836-15]
FOLK, Charles 161
FORBES, James 5, 57, 133
FORBUSH, James 65, 205
FORD, Thos. 215
FORE
    A.P. 39, 55, 174, 221, [1836-7], [1836-12], [1836-13], [1836-14], [1836-17]
FORESTER
    Wm. 47, 112, 169, 188
FORGY, Andrew 163, 192, 205
FORREST, FORRIST
    James [1836-5]
    William L. [1836-10]
FORSTER
    John & Chrisley [1836-1]
    Thomas [1836-1]
    William [1836-1]
FORTNER, William [1836-1]
FOSTER, Andrew [1836-1]
    Anthonny (Anthony) 35, [1836-12]
    Benjamin [1836-4]
    Daniel 18, 57, 172
    Frederick [1836-9]
    Garret (Garnet, Jerrod) 11, 60, 126, 222

George 22
John & Chrisley 26, 70, 120, 177
Levi 91
Simpson 18, 75, 224, [1836-12]
Thomas 3, 91, 138, 196
Wm. 26, 70, 120, 177
FOUT - See BERRY and FOUT
FOUNKHUSER - See FUNKHOUSER
FOWLER, John 122, 198
FOX
    Abraham (Abraham Sr., Abram Sr.) 42, 108, 218, [1836-17]
    Abraham Jr. (Abram Jr.) 42, 161, 218, [1836-17]
    Anderson [1836-17]
    Anna (Ana) 42, 161
    Jacob's Heirs 108, 218, [1836-17]
FRANKLIN
    Bennet 5, 57, 138, 192, [1836-7]
    D. [1836-4]
    Edmond 5, 57, 136
    John 100, 169, 188, [1836-8]
    Robert 100, 169, 188, [1836-8]
    William [1836-8]
FRAZIER, FRAZURE
    Martin 188, [1836-11]
    Samuel (Saml.) 44, 105, [1836-11]
    Thomas (Thos.) 24, 88, 115, 155, 183, [1836-6]
FREEMAN, Francis 31, 82, 128
    Joel T. 18, 75
    John 9
FRENCH, Gidcon 88, 155, 183
FREEZE, Martin [1836-8]
FRY, Austin 1, 91, [1836-1]
    Harvey, (Hary, Henry) 1, 84, 138, 196
    John (John S.) 91, 151, 200, [1836-1]
    Newell C. [1836-1]
    Philip 1, 91, 151, 200, [1836-1]

FULCHER, Saml. 37, 98
FULLER, Thomas 11
FULTZ, Andrew 35
    Henry 39
FUNKHOUSER, FOUNKHOUSER
    [No name given] 173
    Henry 42, 108
    Jacob 42, 108, 202, [1836-15]
FURGERSON, FURGISON, FURGURSON
    Robert 115
    Wm. 31, 82, 128, 224
FYFFE, Isaac [1836-16]
    Isaac W. 44
    Isaac W's Heirs & Estate 105, 226, 229
    James H. (J.H.) 43, 44, 105, 115, 226, 227, [1836-7]

G

GADDY, Richard [1836-2]
GAGE, Ebenezer [1836-16]
GALLANT, James [1836-2]
    William [1836-2]
GALYON, Thomas 42
GALZANT, James 26, 120, 177
GAMBLE, Adolphus [1836-11]
GANN
    Adam (Adam Sr.) 7, 67, 161, 163
GANT, James [1836-6]
GARDNER, Wm. 67
GARRET, GARET, GARRETT, JARRETT
    Calvin [1836-5]
    Haron 42, 162, 218
    James [1836-6]
    Washington [1836-5]
    Wm. (Wm. Sr.) 115, 227
GARRINGTON-See CARRINGTON
GARRISON, GARRISSON
    Robert 3, 84, 138, 196, [1836-1]
GARVEY, Christopher 144
GASS, Allen [1836-4]

Allen G. [1836-8]
John (2) [1836-4]
GASTON, GHASTON, GASTIN, GHASTIN
    Joseph 15, 77, 130, 210, [1836-8]
    Thomas 130, 210
GATT, GAUTT, GAULT
    James 35, 65, 133, 205
    Saml. M. 44, 105, 115, 227
GAUNCE, Abraham [1836-2]
GEE, GHEE
    Chas. W. 5, 77, 163, 190
    Hiram (Hiram C.) 20, 144, 202, [1836-14]
    John 20, 163, 190, [1836-11], [1836-14]
    John H. 144, 202
    John M. 20
GENTRY, JENTRY
    Allen 31, 82, 128
    David 82
    James O. [1836-16]
    Samuel [1836-13]
    Shederick 40, 60
GEORGE
    Isaac 15, 100, 169, 227
    Wm. 3, 84, 173, 196
GERIN, GEARON, GHEREN?
    Thomas 3, 84, 109, 196
GETTYS
    James 44, 105, 115, 226, [1836-7]
GHASTON - See GASTON
GHEE - See GEE
GHEST, Richard 115
GHERON - See GERIN
GIBBS
    Flemming (Fleming) 7, 67, 163, 190, [1836-11]
    John M. [1836-7], [1836-14]
    Richard 20, 214, [1836-14]
GIBSON, GIPSON
    George 151, 200, [1836-5]
    James 161
    John [1836-8], [1836-11]
    Jorden 140, 215 (See Jordan Grisham)
    Mathew R. 29, 85, 118, 208, [1836-10]
    Robert [1836-5]
    Thomas 42, 108, 161, 173, 218, [1836-15]
    Wm. C. (Wm.) 29, 67, 86, 118, 208, [1836-11]
GILBERT, Joseph 15
GILBREATH, GILLBREATH
    Elizabeth [1836-14]
    Joseph's Heirs 20, 73, 147, 214
    Thomas (Thos.) 20, 73, 147, [1836-14]
GILL, Saml. 142
    Wm. 39
GILLEHAN - See GILLIAN
GILLELAND, GILLILAND
    Daniel 118, [1836-10]
GILLENWATERS
    Elijah 62, 108, 202, [1836-17]
GILLIAN, GILLEHAN, GILHAN
    Hiram 95, 124
    Magor (Magor M.) 49, 98, 166
    Moses 181
GIPSON - See GIBSON
GIVENS, Joseph 123
GLADEN, GLADDEN, John 142
    Wm. 151, 200
GLASE, GLAZE
    George 151, 200
    George H. [1836-12]
    Henry 1, 91, 151, 200, [1836-1]
    John [1836-1]
    William S. [1836-12]
GLASS, James 147, 214
GLEN, Austin 224
GLOWER, James 70
GODARD, GODDARD
    Hugh 1, [1836-5]
    Hugh & Thornton 91, 151, 200
    Thornton 1, [1836-5]
GOFF, GAUF
    Thomas 39, 55, 142
GOLDING, GOLDIN, GOLDEN

Abraham 27, 70, 177, [1836-2]
Jacob 26, 70, 120, 177, [1836-1]
William [1836-1]
GOLEHAM, Isaac [1836-4]
GOLLYS, James [1836-3]
GONCE
   Abraham 24, 88, 155, 183
   John 24, 88, 155
GOOD, GOODE, Edward [1836-12]
   Hesekiah M. 7
   John 18, 35, 65, 75, 133, 205, [1836-12]
   Wm. 7, 67, 163
GOODWIN, GOODWINE
   James 172, [1836-4]
   L. [1836-16]
   Walker 172
GORD, Miles [1836-4]
GORDEN, John [1836-17]
GOSAGE, Thomas 71, 120, 177
GOSS
   Allen G. (Allen P.) 3, 84, 138, 196
   John 3, 84, 138, 196
GOUSBY, Samuel 194
GRANTHAM
   John 27, 70, 120, 177
GRAVES
   Christopher (Christian) 12, 60, 123, 198, [1836-9]
GRAY, Hugh 118
GREEN, Alexander [1836-14]
   Daniel 161
   Henry 133
   James 18, 75
   James C. 123, 198
   James S. 73, 147, 214, [1836-14]
   John 73, 147, 214
   Reynolds 26
   Richard [1836-15]
   Syrus [1836-11]
   Wm. E. 35, 111, 205
   William H. [1836-3]
GREENWAY, GREINWAY
   David 7, 67, 163, 190, [1836-11]
   James 163
GREENWOOD
   Hudson (Hutson) 39, 59, 146
   John 39, 59, 146
GREEG - See also GRIGG
   James (J.) 12, 60 (2), 110, 122, 123, 198 (2)
GREER, GREEAR
   David 60, 123
GREGORY, John [1836-13]
   Robert 224, [1836-6]
   Tapley 22, 93, 148, 179, [1836-8]
GREINWAY - See GREENWAY
GRIFFIN, James [1836-11]
   Oswell 5, 57, 136, 192
   William [1836-11]
   Wm. Jr. 5, 57, 136, 192
   Wm. Sr. 5, 57, 136, 192
   Young H. 192, [1836-11]
GRIFFITH
   Benjamin 1, 91, 151, 215
   John [1836-16]
   John S. [1836-12]
   William (Wm.) 49, 166, 219, [1836-16]
GRIFFY, James 188
   William 98
GRIGG
   Joel 20, 62, 144, 202, [1836-14]
GRIGSBY, John 183
GRILLS
   Thomas (Thos. J.) 5, 57, 136, 192, [1836-15]
GRIMES, GRYMES
   Hugh 44, 105, 227
GRISHAM, GRISSOM
   Elijah 47, 100, 169, 188, [1836-8]
   J. 172
   James 15, 77, 135, 179
   Jesse (Jesse Esquire) 14, 130, 134, [1836-8]
   Jesse Jr. 15, 77, 135, 179

Jesse Sr. 15, 77, 130, 179
John 9, 102, 140, 190, 215, [1836-3]
Jorden (written Jorden Grisham but I think it should be Jorden Gibson) 102
Michael 9, 102, 215, [1836-3]
Nicholas 140
Simeon 84, 138, 196, [1836-4]
Thomas [1836-1]
Wm. 7, 163
Wm. T's Executors 67
GROGEN, GROGINS, GROGAN
Albert [1836-12]
Wilford (Willford) 144, 202
GRUBB, Amber 123
GRUBLE, William [1836-4]
GRYMES - See GRIMES
GUINN, GUEN, GWINN
Joshua 22, 93, 148, 194, [1836-9]
GUSTY, John 218
GUTHRIE, GUTHREY, GUTHAREY, GOTHERRIE
Thomas 47, 100, 169, [1836-3]
GWINN - See GUINN

H

HACKLER
George 27, 71, 120, 178, [1836-2]
John [1836-2]
Robert 178, [1836-2]
HACKWORTH
Henry 12, 60, 123, 198
HADLEY, John 198
HAFLEY, HAFELEY, KAFELY
Cornelius 47, 101, 140, 215
David 29, 86
HAGGARD, Richard [1836-8]
HAGLER
Abraham W. (A.W.) 37, 95, 124, 181
HALE, HAIL, HAILE

Archibald [1836-11]
Catharine 24, 88
Christopher 5, 57, 136, 205
Franklin [1836-4]
Frederick 24, 88, 155, 183, [1836-11]
James [1836-8]
Lewis [1836-6], [1836-8]
Martin [1836-8]
Samuel (Saml.) 24, 88, 156, 183, [1836-5]
Wm. 123, 126, 153, 207, 222
HALL, Elijah 33
James 49
John W. 108, 218
Joseph F. 27, 71, 120
Nathaniel [1836-6]
Wm. 198
HAMBLETON - See HAMILTON
HAMBRICK
Jeremiah 22, 101, 135, 179
Vinsunt (Vincent) 47, 101, 169
HAMBRIE, Jeremiah [1836-8]
HAMBRIGHT
Amos 98, 166, 230
Benjamin (Benjn.) 49, 98, 166, 181, [1836-16]
Frederick (Frederic) 49, 98, 166, 219, [1836-17]
Given R (G.R.) 49, 98, 166, 181, [1836-16]
John (John Jr.) 49, 98, 166, 219, [1836-16]
John Sr. 49
Heirs of Jo. 98
Nancy 166, 219, [1836-16]
Peter (P.) 49 (2), 98 (2), 166, 219 (2), [1836-16]
William [1836-16]
HAMBY, Adam [1836-13]
Andrew 31
Isacz 49, 98
Jesse [1836-15]
John 37, 95, 124
Joseph 98, 166, 219
Michael 219

Needom [1836-13] (2)
HAMILTON, HAMBLETON
　Albert 163
　Elijah 3, 84, 173, 196
　Henry [1836-11]
　Jesse 7, 67, 163, 190, [1836-15]
　Joseph [1836-6]
　Joshua 208, [1836-10]
　Robert W. 131
　Robt. [1836-11]
HAMMONS, Elisha [1836-6]
HAMPTON, Francis 144, 202
　James 65, 167, 219
　Preston 144
　Wade (Wayde) 49, 98, 124, 219, [1836-16]
　Wm. 49, 98 (2)
　Wm. Jr. 167, 219
　Zachariah 15, [1836-3], [1836-9]
HANCE, Washington 7
HANCOCK, Martin [1836-1]
HAND, HAN
　Elijah [1836-7]
　James (James C) 35, 65, 172, 205, [1836-11]
HANEY, HAYNE, HANIE, HAYNIE
　[No name given] 18
　Emanuel 93, 149, 194, [1836-9], [1836-10]
　Harrel B. [1836-17]
　John [1836-2]
　John Jr. 27
　Martin 75, 159
　Robert 57, 136, 192, [1836-16]
　Stephen [1836-2]
　William 42, 144, 207, 218
　William S. (Wm. S.) 33, 80, 153, [1836-5], [1836-6]
　Willis [1836-9]
HANKS, David 163, 167, 219
　John 49, 98, 167, 219, [1836-15]
HANNAH, HANNAR
　Joseph (Joseph M.) 24, 156, 207

Joshua (Joshua H.) 103, 140
Robert 140
Wm. W. 9
HARDEN, HARDIN
　Ardel [1836-11]
　Elie [1836-9]
　Hardy 3, 84
　Heirs of Hardy (H.) 138, 196
　Joseph [1836-1], [1836-2]
　Joseph (Joseph Jr.) 3, 71, 120, 198
　Joseph (Joseph Sr.) 27, 71, 120, 178
　M. [1836-4]
　Richard 161
　Solomon 3, [1836-9]
　William [1836-9]
HARDWICK, Charles [1836-9]
　John [1836-9]
HARDY
　James [1836-6]
　Samuel (Saml.) 35, 65, 133, 205, [1836-6]
　Stewart 144, 202
　Thomas [1836-15]
　William B. (Wm. B.) 21, 62 (2), [1836-14]
HARKRIDER
　David 78, 110, 135, 179
　George [1836-10]
　John 15, 78, 135, 179, [1836-8]
HARLESS, Jno. 151, 200
HARMON, Jacob [1836-2]
　Leonard [1836-2]
HARNY
　(In the H index) Bradford's Harny (a Horse) 105
HARRELL, HERREL, HERALD, HARREL, HARRIL, HARROLL
　Elijah 133, 188
　Enoch 33, 80, 153, 207, [1836-6]
　Jacob 33, 80, 153
　John [1836-6]
　John Jr. 33, 80, 153, 207
　John Sr. 35, 80, 153

Wiley B. 33
Wm. 35, 133
HARRELSON, HARELSON,
   HERRILSON, HARRIS
   [No name given] 169
   Irvin 24
   James G., Jr. (James G) 98,
      142, 219
   James G., Sr. (James) 167, 219
   Merredith 156
   Peter 163, 227
   Wm. 73, 142, 202
HARRELSTON, William [1836-1]
HARRIS - See also HARRELSON
   George 98, [1836-14]
   John [1836-15]
   William [1836-17]
HARRISSON, HARISON
   Charles 44
   Daniel 42, 108, 161, 218
   Pledge 4, 84, 138, 196
   Richard 42, 108, 161, 218
HARSLER, HOSTLER
   John 98, 167, 219
HART, HEART
   John 9, 103, 140, 215
   John P. [1836-3]
   John Sr. [1836-3]
HARTLEY
   John (Jno.) 151, 200, [1836-5]
   Lorenzo (Lorrensy D.) 151,
      [1836-5]
HARVIE, Ridden [1836-3]
HARWOOD, Zachariah 219
HASKINS, HASHKINS, HESKINS
   Dennis 42, 108, 161, 218,
      [1836-17]
HASTON, Isaac 91, 151, 200
HATFIELD
   Joseph 10, 102, 172, 215
   Valentine 120, 178
HAVENS
   Charles 22, 93, 135, 149, 194
   Hiram 135, [1836-8]
   John 173
HAVID, Ridden [1836-3]

HAWK, John 161
   Madison C. [1836-16]
HAWKS, William [1836-1]
HAWKINS
   Benjamin 29, 86, 118, 208
   David 82
   James 22, 47, 110, 126, 222,
      [1836-9], [1836-17]
   James' Admn. 47
   John 12, 118, 222
   Joseph 29, 224, [1836-6]
   Raleigh 12
   Right 22, 78
   William 109
HAYMES
   Caleb 15, 78, 130, 210, [1836-
      11]
   Daniel [1836-11]
   David 118, 210 (written Haynes
      on 118), [1836-11]
   Jane [1836-11]
   Joshua [1836-11]
   Vincent 15, 77, 130, 210,
      [1836-11]
   William [1836-11]
   Wm. (Wm. Sr.) 78, 130, 210
   Wm. Jr. 130, 210
HAYNES, HANES
   Aaron 11, 12, 60, 128, 224,
      [1836-9]
   Christopher 12, 124
   George M. (Geo. M.) 95, [1836-
      9]
   James [1836-9]
   John 12, 110, 194
   Joseph 88, 123, 198
HAYS, HAYES, HAYSE, HASE
   Absolem (Absalem, Absolom
      C) 15, 77, 172, 190, [1836-
      11]
   James 47, 101, 130, 169, 188,
      205, [1836-3], [1836-8]
   John (John F.) 35, 65, 133, 205,
      [1836-16]
   Samuel 205

Solomon 22, 93, 148, 172, 194,
[1836-8]
William 183, 210
William B. Sr. (Wm. B.) 210,
[1836-11]
HAZARD, HAZZARD
Richd. 135, 179
HEADERICK, HEDRICK, HEDERICK,
HADRICK
Henry 153
Wm. 33, 80, 153, 207
HEAFTEY, Cornelius, [1836-8]
HEAGHART - See HUGHART
HEARD, HERD, HURD
Abraham A. (A. A.) 21, 62, 173
Heirs of Abrm. (A) 21, 62, 144,
202, [1836-17]
Rebecca 24, 88
HEARLSON, HIRELSTON
James 3
Wm. 27, 65, 71, 120, 178, 205
HEATH, Elias 35
HEDERICK - See HEADERICK
HEDRICK - See HEADERICK
HENRY, Bartholomew [1836-12]
HELMS, HELLEMS, HELMES
J.C. [1836-16]
James 49, 98, 167, 219
John 49, 166, 219, [1836-16]
Joseph S. [1836-16]
Thomas [1836-16]
William (Wm.) 49, 98, 166,
219, [1836-16]
HELTERBRAND, Michael 42
HELTON, Peter 82, 128
Wiley [1836-12]
Wm. 207
HELVEY
Andrew 22, 93, 149, 194,
[1836-8]
Daniel U. [1836-8]
HEMPHILL, James [1836-7]
John 4, 138, 196
Thomas 85, 138, 196
HENDERSON, Allen 123, 198
C.S. [1836-5]

George [1836-9]
Isaac 39, 59, 146, 212
James 31, 59, 146, 212
John C. [1836-17]
Mary [1836-17]
William (Wm.) 12, 22, 60, 93,
123, 146, 198, 212, [1836-9]
William C. [1836-17]
HENLY
James D. (J. D.) 22 (2), 93 (2),
111, 148, 179 (2), [1836-8]
HENNIGER, Henry [1836-7]
HENRY
Bartholomew (Bartley) 18, 75,
187
Wm. 62
HENTZ, A.H. [1836-8]
HERALD - See HARRELL
HERD - See HEARD
HEROD, Redden 10
HERREL - See HARRELL
HERRILSON - See HARRELSON
HERRON, Wm. M. 227
HESKINS - See HASKINS
HESTER, HESTRE, HESTOR
Abraham [1836-12], [1836-13]
Charles 39, 59
Isaac 59, 159
HIATT, HYOTT
Jobe (Job) 115, 227, [1836-7]
HIGHDON - See HIDEN
HICKEY, HICEY, HICKY
James 29, 47, 86, 118, 208,
[1836-10], [1836-16]
HICKLIN, HICKLEN
Barnet (Barney) 29, 86, 181,
[1836-10]
HICKMAN, Frederick 15, 78
Isaac (Isach) 47, 110, 215
J. 101
John 109, 179, [1836-8]
Samuel L. [1836-2]
Thos. 9, 101, 140
William [1836-8]
HICKOX, Heirs [1836-15]

Horace 44, 105, 172, 226, 227
HICKS, HIX, Abraham [1836-10]
    Charles [1836-8]
    Douthat 207
    Garret 153, 207
    George 31
    Gilbert 207
    Isaac [1836-6]
    James 27, 71, 111, 120, 167, 178, [1836-2], [1836-4]
    John (Jno.) 151, 200, [1836-5]
    Martin M. [1836-6]
    Merida 207
    Richard N. 49, 167, 219
    Shederick (Shadrick) 33, 80, 153, 207, [1836-6]
    Stephen [1836-1]
    Timothy 188
HICKY - See HICKEY
HIDEN, HIGHDON, David 31, 82
    Thomas 35, 65
HIDER, James 31
    Joseph 31, 82
    Wm. 82
HIGGINS, Abel 44
    Enuch 219
HIGHSAW, HISAW
    Joseph 39, 59, 148, 212
HIGHTOWER
    Wm. 44, 105, 156, 183, [1836-5]
HILL, Captain 1
    Claiborne (Claborn) 1, 91, 151, 200, [1836-4]
    Isaac 1, 91, 151, 200, [1836-5]
    Joab (Joabb) 1 (2), 91 (2), 151, 200 (2), [1836-4], [1836-5]
    John 31, 82 (2), 128, 173, 224 (2), [1836-6], [1836-12]
    Plesant 200
    Saml. 24
    Thomas [1836-5]
    William (Wm.) 31, 151, 200, [1836-4], [1836-5]
HINES, Zachariah 15, 135
HINKLE, Edward (Edwin) 57, 136

    Jesse 5, 57, 136, 192, [1836-11]
    Philip 57, 172, 192
HISAW - See HIGHSAW
HIX - See HICKS
HOARD - See HORD
HOBACK, Jacob 115
HODGES, HODGE
    Anderson [1836-3]
    Thomas 3, 85, 120, 178
HOGAN, Wm. 44, 103, 115
HOGUE, Heirs of B. H. 44, 105, 115
    Patsy 53
HOIL - See HOYLE
HOLLOWAY, HOLEWAY
    Saml. 10, 103, 140, 215
HOLT, Francis 200
    Francis A. 200, [1836-5]
    Irby's Heirs 151
    James 200
    Jane [1836-5]
    Robert S. 200
    Sarah (Sarrah) 1, 91, 151, 200, [1836-5]
    Serena 200, [1836-5]
    Thomas [1836-5]
    Thomas W. 200
HOOD
    Arthur [1836-8]
    Harthem (Arthem) 22, 149, 179
    John 4, 85, 138
    Jonathan 102
    Joseph C.S. (Joseph) 44, 105, 115, 227
    P.C.S. [1836-17]
    Robert 62, 144, 202
    Saml. 44, 105, 115, 227
    Wm. 4, 85, 138
HOOPER
    Andrew 12, 60, 123, 198, [1836-9]
    Augustus [1836-14]
    Wm. A. 40, 59, 146, 212
    William [1836-13]
HOOSONG, James 15, 78
HOPE

James (James W.) 44, 105, 115, 227
HOPKINS, Daniel 39
  John A. 59
  Thomas heirs [1836-7]
HOPPER, Augustine 202
  John 42
HORD, HOARD
  Eldridge, Gdn. of S. H. Hord Heirs 62
  Standwix Heirs (S. Heirs, Stanwie Heirs) 21, 144, 202, [1836-17]
  Thos. 21, 62, 202
HORKEMAN, William [1836-8]
HORN, HORNE, David 10
  George 105, 115, 227, [1836-7]
  Joshua 10
  Riley 47, 105, 147, 214
  West W. 147
  Wm. 37, 95, 140
HORTON, Daniel [1836-8]
HOSS, Elkanah 105, 115
  Jacob 44, 105, 115, 227, [1836-15]
HOSTLER - See HARSLER
HOUSER, Jefferson H. 224
HOWARD, George 44, 105
  Henry 93
  John 115, 227, [1836-7]
  Thomas 39, 59, 143, 221, [1836-14]
  Wm. 93
HOWELL, HOWEL
  James 1, 91, 151, 200, [1836-1]
  John 4, 10, 102, 194
  Robert 42, 108, 162
  William [1836-17]
HOY, James 227
HOYLE, HOIL, HOILE
  Andrew [1836-14]
  Claton 27
  David 18, 75, 159, 187, [1836-14]
  Joel 40, 55, 143

John 39, 55, 143, 221, [1836-14]
Jonas 221, [1836-14]
Levi 39, 111
Peter (Peter, Jr.) 18, 159, 187, 221, [1836-14]
Thomas L. (Thomas) 18, 73, 142, 221, [1836-14]
HUDGINS, Josiah 21, 62, 144, 202
HUDNELL, Mary 29, 86, 118
HUDSON - See HUTSON
HUFFAKER, HUFAKER
  Benj. [1836-14]
  Christopher 21, 73, 147, 214, [1836-14]
  Isaac 37, 95, 124, 208
  James [1836-10]
  Lewis 39, 55, 143, 221, [1836-14]
HUGHART, HEAGHART
  Wm. 12, 60, 194
HUGHBANK George [1836-1]
HUGHS, HUGHES
  Jacob 40, 55, 143
  Leander 15, 77, 130
  Meredith 40
  Prior 166, 219, [1836-15]
HULL, Lewis 37
HUMPHREYS, HUMPHRES, HUMPHREY
  Hilton (H.) 44, 105, 172, [1836-7]
  John (Jn.) 210, [1836-4]
HUNT
  Elijah [1836-7]
  Grandeson, (Grandason, Granderson) 15, 78, 130, 210, [1836-11]
  John [1836-10]
  L.L. [1836-8]
  Levi B. [1836-13]
  Martin 135
HUNTER
  William (Wm.) 123, 198, [1836-9]
HURD - See HEARD

HURST
    Elijah 1, 91, 113, 115, 151, 172, 227, [1836-4]
    John L. [1836-4]
    Russell 115, 200, [1836-4]
HUTCHESON, Lewis B. 224
    Saml. 71, 120
HUTSEL, Andrew [1836-7]
HUTSON, HUDSON
    Robert B. 188, [1836-3]
HYOTT - See HIATT

I

INSLEY - See ENSLY
INGRAM, George [1836-10]
IRELAND, Jonathan 40
    Thomas 184
ISAACS, C.W. [1836-4]
ISBELL
    Benjamin (Benj.) 24 (2), 89, 155, 156, 184, [1836-5]
ISEBY, George [1836-15]
ISHAM, ISOM
    Bolen (Bolin) 215, [1836-3]
    Charles 53, 103, 140, 215, [1836-3]
    James [1836-9]
    John 101, 103, 169, 215, [1836-3]
    William 215, [1836-3]
IRWIN - See ERWIN
IRVIN - See ERWIN
IVY, IVEY, Ausley [1836-2]
    Curtis 27, 71, 120
    Hartwell 27, 71, 120, 178, [1836-2]

J

JACK, James [1836-12]
    Jeremiah 227
    John 82, 224, [1836-13]
    Mary 83, 224, [1836-12]
    Samuel 224
    Wm. 32
JACKSON, James 33, 82
    John 18, 32, 75, 159, 187, 224
    Heirs of John 212
    John B. 15, 78, 131, 210, [1836-7]
    John K. [1836-12]
    R. G. 115, 227
    Richard C. [1836-7]
    Woody [1836-17]
JACKSON & McCONNEL [1836-17]
JAMERSON - See JAMISON
JAMES, Edward 27
    Isom [1836-9]
    John 71, 120
    Joshua 167, 220
JAMISON, JEMISON, JAMERSON
    Benjamin 12, 123, 198
    Benjamin C. [1836-9]
    David F. 4, 85, 138, 197, [1836-1]
    Elizabeth [1836-9]
    James M. 198
    Joshua R. 178
    Saml. 37, 96, 126
    Thomas [1836-12]
JANUARY, John 33, 224
JARNAGIN, JERNEGAN, JOURNAGAN, JOURNEGAN, JONIGAN
    Coswell (Caswell) 53, 109, 131, 210, [1836-11]
    Wm. 131, 210
JARRETT - See GARRETT
JEMISON - See JAMISON
JENKINS, JENKENS, JINKINS
    David 50, 112, 167
    James 181
    John [1836-16]
    Wm. 135
JENTRY - See GENTRY
JERREL, John F. [1836-10]
JILES, William [1836-17]
JINKINS - See JENKINS

JOHN, JOHNS
    Andrew (Andy) 115, 156, [1836-5]
    Ezekial, Jr. (Ezekiel) 156, 184, [1836-4]
    Hugh [1836-11]
    Robert 24, 89, 156, 184, [1836-5]
    Saml. 115
    Thomas 24, 89, 156, 184, [1836-4], [1836-5]
    William (Wm.) (JOHN) 24, 89, 156, 184, [1836-5]
    Wm. (JOHNS) 29, 222
JOHNSON, JOHNSTON
    Ashael, (Asael) 44, 105
    Henry [1836-2]
    Hudson (Hutson) 29, 86, 118, 208, [1836-11]
    Jacob 7, 67
    James 96, 115, 124, 181
    Jarrett (Jaret) 18, 75, [1836-11]
    Joel 99, 167, 220, [1836-16]
    John [1836-9]
    Joseph 50, 190
    Lewis 50, 99, 167, 220, [1836-16]
    Madison [1836-4]
    Mary (Polly) 50, 83, 99, 167
    Reubin (R.) Heirs of, 7, 67, 164
    Saml. 44, 92, 151, 200, [1836-4]
    Shaderick 32
    Theodore P. (Theo. P.) 115, 227, [1836-7]
    Thomas 138
    Urial 44, 105, 114, 115, 227, [1836-7]
    William (Wm.) 50, 99, 167, 220, [1836-10] (2), [1836-16]
    Wm. J. 222
    W.S. [1836-16]
JOLLY
    Henry (Henry H.) 42, 108, 162, 218

JONES, Albin 44, 105, 115, 227
    Biram 200
    Isaac 50, 99, 167, 220
    James 49, 99, 167, 220
    Joel 4, 85, 138, 197
    John 156, 184
    Reese (Reace, Reece) 22, 172, 190, [1836-15], [1836-16]
    Samuel [1836-15]
    Steven [1836-11]
    Thomas 108, 110, 162, 218
    William (Wm.) 22, 40, 49, 55, 99, 111, 126, 149, 190, 197, 222, [1836-2], [1836-10], [1836-16]
    Wm. (Wm. Sr.) 4, 85, 138, 197
    Wm. B. 164, 190
    William Jr. [1836-3]
JONIGAN - See JARNAGIN
JORDEN, JORDAN
    Robt. H. 105, 151, 200
    Robt. W. [1836-3]
    Samuel H. (S. H.) 105, 115, 227, [1836-7]
JOURNAGAN - See JARNAGIN
JOURNEGAN - See JARNAGIN
JULIAN, George [1836-6]
    James [1836-11]
    Isom [1836-6]

K

KAFELY - See HAFLY
KAIN - See CAIN
KANADY - See KENNEDY
KARR, KERR, KEAR
    James 190, 194, [1836-16]
    William (Wm., Wm. Jr.) 40, 55, 110, 123, 143 (2), 199, 221, 230, [1836-9]
KEAN - See CAIN
KEAR - See KARR
KEATH - See KEITH
KEELIN, Wm. 62
KEETON, Littleton [1836-4]

William [1836-4]
KEITH, KEATH, KIETH
    Alexander [1836-7]
    Chas. F. (C. F.) 24, 105, 115, 227, [1836-4], [1836-7]
    Cornelius 169
    Martin 227
    Nicholas (Nicelous) 101, 201
    Partrick P. [1836-4]
    Zachariah (Zachorah) 101, 169, 201, [1836-17]
KELLY, Daniel 83, 129, [1836-13]
    Joel 35, 65, 133, 205
    Joel, Jr. 44, 105
    John 32, 65, 83, 128, 133, 212
    Jonathan 35, 65, [1836-13]
    Mathew 35 (2), 162
    Mathew, Sr. 44, 105, 115, 227
    Nathen (Nathan) 133, [1836-13]
    Nathan R. [1836-13]
    Richard 35, 65, 105, 129, 133, 205, 212, [1836-7], [1836-13]
    Samuel 221, [1836-13], [1836-14]
    Squire (Squire R.) 44, 105, 115, 227
    Stephen 44, 105, 115, 227
    William (Wm.) 29, 32, 83 (2), 86, 109, 128, 129, 135, 208, 212 (2), [1836-8], [1836-13]
KENNEDY, KANADY, KENNEDAY, KENEDAY
    Jacob (Jacob W.) 65, 133, 204
    James 27, 71, 120, 144, 178, [1836-2]
    Moses 27, 71
    Nancey (Nancy) 21, [1836-17]
    Pleasant M. [1836-7]
    Samuel 202, [1836-17]
    Thomas R. [1836-2]
KERKSEY - See KIRKSEY
KERR - See KARR
KETEN, Benton [1836-3]
KEY, KEE, John 89, 156, 184

Thomas (Thos.) 24, [1836-5]
William [1836-5]
KEYS
    A. D. 44, 105, 115, 227, [1836-7]
KIBBLE
    John 12, 60, 111, 126, 222, [1836-9]
KIETH - See KEITH
KILLEN, James 42, 108
KILLING, KILLINGSWORTH
    Daniel 224
    John 224
    William Sr. 224
    William Jr. 224
KILLINGSWORTH, Isaac 197
    Joseph [1836-6]
    Ruebin 32, 83, 128, 224
    Wm. 32, 83, 128
KINCANNON, KINCANON
    Andrew 10, 140
    Francis 18, 57, 75, 147, 214
    John 10, 140
KINDER
    Peter 44, 105, 115, 227, [1836-7]
KINDRICK, Francis [1836-7]
    Mrs. (Prankey) 115, 227
KING
    Alfred 24, 89, 156, 184, [1836-5]
    Henry [1836-10]
    John B. 10, 106, 115, [1836-2], [1836-7]
    John M. [1836-16]
    Thomas R. 149
    William (Wm.) 44, 50, 105, 115, 205, [1836-7]
KINMAN
    Claburk (Claibourn, Claborn) 29, 86, 208, 230
    Samuel (Saml.) 29, 86, 118, 208, [1836-10]
    Wesley (Westly) 29, 86, 118, 208

William (Wm.) 29, 86, 118, 208, [1836-10]
KINNARD, CINNARD, CANORD
    George 14, 77, 124, 208
KINSER, Henry [1836-10]
KIRKPATRICK, KIRKPARTRICK
    [No Name Given] 92
    Joel 101, 188
    John 4, 85, 138, 197, [1836-1]
KIRKSEY, KERKSEY
    Christopher 40, 55, 221
    Ed C. 143
    Elisha 40, 55
    George (George W.) 40, 55, 143, 221, [1836-14]
    Thomas [1836-14]
KITCHEN, KITCHENS
    John 120, 169, 178, 188, [1836-2]
    Wm. 47, 188, 197
KITCHERSIDE, Jas. 149
KNIGHT, NIGHT
    Dennis [1836-16]
    William (Wm.) 60, [1836-9]
KNOTT, Robert 149
KNOX, NOX, David L. 202
    James 10, 103, 140, 215, [1836-3]
    John 10, 103, 140, 215
    William (Wm.) 10, 103, 140, 215, [1836-3]

L

LACAS, Robert [1836-1]
LACETER - See LASETER
LACERTER - See LASETER
LACEY, LACY, LASEY
    Lovi (Levi) 4, 111, 138, [1836-1]
    William (Wm.) 4, 85, 138, [1836-2]
LACKEY, LACKY, Hurl? (Hve?) 15
    John 13, 202
    Robert 15

Robt. [1836-11]
LACKLAND, David 25
LACKY - See LACKEY
LADD, Dick (man of color) 62
LAIN - See LANE
LAIRD, David [1836-10]
    Joseph [1836-10]
    Samuel [1836-10]
LAMBERT, John 101, 170, 189
LAND, David 118
LANDRUM, Willis H. 45, 105
LANE, LAIN
    Isaac 2, 92, 151, 200, [1836-4], [1836-5]
    John 2, 152, 200, [1836-4], [1836-5]
    John B. 129, 225
    Lidenae [1836-8]
    Noah 6, 57, 136, 192
    Pleasant W. [1836-8]
    Russell 2, 92, 151, 200, [1836-5]
    Tidonce (Tidence) 47, 101, 170, 189, [1836-5]
    Tidonce C. 4, 85, 138, 197
LANG, John [1836-11]
LANGHAM, Elias [1836-13]
LANGLEY, LANGLY
    James [1836-15]
    Jonathan [1836-10]
LANGSTON, Martin [1836-15]
LANKFORD, LANGFORD
    Gipson 227
    John 40, 55, 143
    Robert 8, 68, 164
LARAMORE - See LARIMORE
LARGE, Isaac [1836-8]
LARGENT, Albert [1836-11]
LARIMORE, LARAMORE
    George K. [1836-17]
    Hugh 8, 68, 164, 191, [1836-11]
    Jno. 115
    Roland 8, 68, 164, 191, [1836-11]
LARISON, LARRISSON, LARASON
    James 103, 141, 216

John F. 216
Peter 22, 93, 148, 195, 215
Wm. I., 103, 215
LARUE, Wm. 8
LASETER, LASITER, LACITER, LACETER, LACERTER
   Jonathan 83, 207, [1836-6]
   Wiley 31, 32, 83, 128, 129, 225, [1836-6]
LASEY - See LACEY
LASLEY - See LESSLEY
LASLY - See LESSLEY
LASTLEY - See LESSLEY
LATHAM, Henry [1836-2]
LATIMORE, John 18, 73, 147, 214
   Samuel 40, 55, 143
   Susannah [1836-14]
LAUGHAM, LAUGAM
   Elias 146, 212
LAUGHTER, Wiley [1836-16]
LAVENDOR, George M. [1836-16]
LAWSON, LOSSON
   A.H. [1836-12]
   Allen 10, 103, 140, 215, [1836-3]
   Andrew [1836-3]
   Asa 93, 141, 216
   David 10, 103, 141, 215
   David (David Jr.) 10, 103, 141, 215, [1836-3]
   David Sr. [1836-3]
   Hugh 10, 103, 141, 215, [1836-3]
   Isham (Isom) 18, 75, 159, 187, [1836-12]
   Jacob 10, 103, 141, 216, 231
   Jacob Jr. 216, [1836-3]
   Jacob Sr. [1836-3]
   James 10, 103, [1836-3]
   Jesse 140
   Jno. F. 141
   Lacy [1836-4]
   Nathan 10, 103, 141, 215
   Nathan Jr. [1836-3]
   Nathan Sr. [1836-3]
   Richard 10, 103, 141, 215, [1836-3]
   Russel [1836-12]
   Tenny (Tiny) 215, [1836-3]
   Type (Tyler) 10, 103
   Wm. 60, 123
   Wm. T. 10, 141
LEADBETTER, John [1836-9]
LEATHERWOOD
   Aquilla 18, 75, 159, 187
   Ruebin 32, 83
LEE, LEA
   Abner 18, 75, 110, 159, 202
   Abner, Jr. 202
   James 126, 222
   Nagor 18, 75
   Marnon ? 154
   Samuel [1836-5]
   William (Wm.) 32, 83, 129 (See Wm. Low 225), [1836-6], [1836-17]
   Young 202
LEGG, LEG, Isaac 47, 101, 169, 188
   Samuel (Saml.) 15, 47, 78, 101, 135, 169, 179, [1836-8]
   Simeon 47, 101, 169, 188
   Wiley (Wiley B.) 101, 169, 188
LEMMONS, LEMON
   Holan (Holdin, Holand) 50, 99, 167, 220, [1836-15]
   John 220
   Levi 50
   Reuben [1836-15]
   Reubin (Reubin Sr.) 50, 99, 167, 220
   Reubin (Reubin Jr.) 50, 99, 167, 220
   William (Wm.) 50, 99, 167, 220, [1836-15]
LEO, Nicholas [1836-16]
LEOMENS, William [1836-16], [1836-17]
LENARD, Joshua 210
LENORE & McPHERSON, 45, 106
LENOAR, LENOR
   James (James B.) 99, 167, 220
   Oswell W. 99, 167, 220

LESSLEY, LESLEY, LESSLY, LASLEY, LASLY, LASTLEY
  James, Sr. 40, 146
  Jesse 29, 110, 199
  Samuel (Saml.) 40, 59, 212, [1836-13]
  Thomas (Thomas Jr.) 40, 59, 146, 212, [1836-13]
  Thomas Sr. 40, 59, 146, 212, [1836-13]
LETT, Ambrose 29, 87, 118, 208
LEWALLEN, LEWELLING, LUALLEN
  Jesse [1836-8]
  Lewis [1836-2]
  Robert [1836-8]
  Wesly 172
  Wiley 103, 215
LEWIS, Edmund [1836-6]
  Jno. (Jno. C.) 126, 222
LILES - See LYLE
LILLARD, James 93, 149, 195
LINDSLEY, LINSLEY
  George W. 33, 80, 155, 207
LINGERFELT, Jacob [1836-14]
LINER, James S. 50
  Oswalt [1836-16]
LINSLEY - See LINDSLEY
LITTERAL, LITERAL
  James-Heirs of 49
  Richard 4, 85
LOCK, [no name] [1836-16]
  John 50, 99, 167
LODGE, Meridian Sun [1836-7]
LOGAN, Abner 147, 214, [1836-12]
  Elizabeth [1836-14]
  John 32, 83, 129
  Wm. 18, 73, 147
LONG, George [1836-15]
  George Jr. 8, 68, 164, 191
  George Sr. 8, 68, 164, 191
  Isaac 191, [1836-15]
  Henry [1836-16]
  James 7, 18, 67, 75, 159, 164, 187, 191, [1836-12]
  Jesse [1836-8]
  John 8, 68, 164, 191
  Maples 164, 191, [1836-15]
  Moses 164, 191, [1836-15]
  Samuel [1836-12], [1836-14]
LONGLEY, James 7, 67, 164, 191
  Joel 8, 68
  John 7, 220
  Jonathan (Johnathan) 29, 87, 118, 208
  Wm. 7, 67, 164
LONGWITH, LONGWITT
  Reuben 15, 192, [1836-11]
LORD, Joseph 118
LOSSON - See LAWSON
LOTSPEACH, LOTSPEICH
  John 71, 120
  Samuel [1836-7]
LOURY - See LOWRY
LOVE, Edward [1836-2]
  Jno. & Thos. B. 147
  John (John M.) 32, 83, 126, 195, [1836-6], [1836-9]
  Robert 12
  Thomas B. (Thos. B.) 42, 73, 147, 214, [1836-15]
  Wm. K. 45, 106
LOVEL, John [1836-12]
LOVEY, Pearson [1836-1]
LOW, LOWE
  Abraham 25, 89, 156, 184
  Isaac 89, 154, 156, [1836-6]
  James 33, 80, 220, [1836-6]
  Michael 32, 83, 146, 225
  William 225 (Possibly William Lee)
LOWRY, LOWERY, LOURY
  Barthy H. [1836-7]
  Daniel 25, 89, 156, 184, [1836-5]
  Isaac 24, 89, 156, 184, [1836-5]
  James 101, 170, 173, 184
  James Jr. 24, 89, 156, 184, [1836-5]
  James Sr. 24, 89, 156, [1836-5]
  James P. 45, 105 (I did not separate the James)
  John 184, [1836-5]

Michael [1836-13]
Sarah 123
Susannah 12, 60
William (Wm.) 45, 104, 105, 115, 227, [1836-7]
LOYD, LOYDE, James [1836-7]
John W. 189, [1836-7]
Thos. 10
LUALLEN - See LEWALLEN
LUCIUS, Thomas 60
LUCK, John [1836-17]
LUCKY, John [1836-17]
LUSK, Hugh [1836-5]
John 25, 89, 156, 184, [1836-5]
Wm. 25
LYLE, LYLES, LILES
Martha 85, 138, 197, [1836-4]
James H. (James L.) 15, 78, 131, 191
LYNDEN, Abraham 21

M

McADOO
Richard L. (Richd.) 135, 179
McALESTER, McALLISTER, McCALLESTER, McCALLISTER, McCALISTER
Jas. 167
Jesse 50, 99, 167
John 50, 99
Wesley 50, 99, 167, [1836-15], [1836-16]
William 99, 167
McALLEN, McCALAND, McCALLON
James 211
John 36, 65, 159, 205
McANALLY, Charles [1836-10]
McBEE, Alexander [1836-5]
Wm. 68, 164
McBREAN, McBREEAN, McBRIER
William (Wm. S.) 40, 55, 143, 221, [1836-14]
McCAINE, Jno. 109
McCALAND - See McALLEN

McCALL, McCOLL
Duncan (Dunking) 4, 27, 71
John 4, 85, 139, 178
Sarah 120, 178, [1836-1], [1836-2]
Solomon 71, 120
McCALLIE
William T. (Wm. T.) 37, 96, 124, 181, [1836-16]
McCALLON - See McALLEN
McCAMEY - See McKAMEY
McCAMISH, McCAMMISH
John 2, 92
McCAMMAN, Elizabeth C. [1836-10]
McCANN, James 195, [1836-8]
McCARMIE, Stephen [1836-17]
McCARTNEY
James 42, 99, 166, 167
John Jr. (John) 42, 162, 220, [1836-17]
John Sr. 109, 162, 218, [1836-17]
McCARTY
John L. 37, 96, 125, 181, [1836-10]
McGee & McCarty [1836-16]
McCASLIN, McCASLAND
James 48, 101
McCHRISTEN, Robert [1836-3]
McCLAIN - See Also McLAIR
Robert 30, 87, 118
McCLARREN - See McLARRAN
McCLARY, McCLEARY
James [1836-1]
Robert W. (Robt. W.) 21, 73, 147, [1836-15]
McCLATCHEY, McCLATCHY
Adolphis P. (A.P., A. D. P.) 38, 96, 125, 181, [1836-16]
John 37, 96, 125, 181, [1836-16]
McCLEARY - See McCLARY
McCLELAN, John 38
McCLURE, Halbert 15, 78, 116, 228
McCOLL - See McCALL
McCOMICK, McCOMMICK

Benjamin 2, 92, 152
McCONNELL, McCONELL,
McCONNALL - See also JACKSON
  Alexander 45, 106
  Charles [1836-10]
  Joseph (Joseph S) 38, 96, 124,
    182, [1836-16]
  Samuel (Saml.) 41, 42, 108,
    109, 218, [1836-17]
McCOY
  Birdine (Birdon, Burden) 8, 68,
    164, 211, [1836-11]
  Daniel 80, 121, 153, 207,
    [1836-2]
  Heirs [1836-16]
  Robert W. 214
  Wm., Heirs of 44
McCRAY, McRAY, Curtis 92
  Wm. (Wm. M.) 8, 68
McCROSKEY, McCROSKY
  Robert 58, 136, 192, [1836-15]
McCROY, Charles [1836-5]
McCULLY
  Alexander 85, 139, 197, [1836-
    1]
  George 30, 87, 118, 208, [1836-
    10]
  Joseph 87, 118, [1836-10]
McDANIEL, McDANALL
  Alexandria 25, 89
  Charles W. [1836-8]
  George W. 159
  John [1836-16]
  John W. 187
  Washington 18, 76
  Wm. 50, 76, 220, [1836-5]
McDEUGAL - See McDOUGALD
McDONALD, McDONAL,
McDONNALD
  Hugh [1836-11]
  James 6, 68, 110, 164
  John 211, [1836-11]
McDOW, David 187
  John 6, 58
McDOWEL, McDOWALL,
McDOWELL?, McDOWAL

Isaac 12, 60, 123, 222
John [1836-16]
John Jr. 12, 60, 126, 222
John Sr. (John) 12, 37, 60, 127,
  199
McDOUGALD, McDUGALD,
McDOUGLE, McDEUGAL
  Malcolm (Malcon, Malker,
    Malcom) 15, 48, 78, 131,
    211 [1836-11]
McEWIN & McKAMEY HEIRS- 45,
  106
McGAHY, John [1836-7]
  Robert [1836-7]
McGEE, McGHEE
  Daniel H. [1836-12]
  David 37
  George 45, 106
  James 37
  John [1836-5]
  McGee & McCarty [1836-16]
McGOWAN, McGOWEN
  Francis 18, 75, 159, 187, [1836-
    14]
McGUIRE, Henry [1836-6]
  William [1836-16]
McINTURFF
  David 12, 110, 126, 222
  John Sr. (John) 12, 60, 110,
    126, 222
  Sam C. 222
  Thomas (Thos.) 12, 110, 126,
    222, [1836-9]
McKAMEY & McEWIN
  45, 106
McKAMEY, McKAMY, McCAMEY
  [no name] 50, 112, 118
  William [1836-16]
McKEAL - See McKEEL
McKEEHEN, McKEHAN, McKEEHAN
  Aron 25, 89, 157, 184, [1836-5]
  George H. [1836-6]
  James 25, 89, 157, [1836-5]
  Job (Jobe) 25, 89, 156, 184,
    [1836-5]
McKEEL, McKEAL

Singleton 12, 60, 110, 123, 199
McKELDIN, A.M. & Co [1836-7]
McKENNY - See McKINNEY
McKINNEY, McKINEY, McKINNY, McKENNY
   Barnacus [1836-11]
   George 212
   Nathl. 106, 115, 228
   Wm. [1836-11]
McKNIGHT - See McNIGHT
McLAIR, McCLAIN? Jno. 129
McLARRAN, McCLARREN
   Hugh 4, 85, 138, 197
McLILLARD, McLELLARD, McLEALARD
   John 85, 125, 182
McMAHAN
   Caswell 36, 65, 133, 205
   Elizabeth [1836-11]
   James 36, 65, 133, 205
   John 35, 53, 101, 170, 189, [1836-3]
   Washington (Washington C. W.) 65, 133, 205
   Wm. L. 126, 222
McMILLIN, McMILLIAN, McMILLON, McMILLION
   Joseph W. (J. W., Joseph) 29, 30, 86, 87,118, 208, 228
   Wm. 30, 87, 118, 208
McMINN, George 125, 181
   John Jr. 96, 181 (on page 125 there is John Jr. who is evidently John Sr.)
   John Sr. (John) 96, 125, 181
McNABB
   James 23, 94, 149, 195, [1836-8], [1836-10]
   Mathew 42, 109, 162
   William [1836-8]
McNEALLY, Frisser 15
McNIGHT, McKNIGHT, 8, 68, 164, 191
   Robt. [1836-11]
   Saml. 37, 99
McPHAIL, McPHALE
   Daniel 27, 71, 120, 178, [1836-2]
   Dugal (Dugald) 27, 71, 120, 178, [1836-2]
   John 27, 71, 120, 178, [1836-2]
   Niel (Neil) 27, 71, 120, 178, [1836-2]
McPHERSON, Alexander 85, 139
   Ann [1836-4]
   Barton 4, 85, 139, 197
   Geo. 139
   Joseph 116, 228
   Richard 37
   Widow [1836-4]
McPHERSON & ZENORE 45, 106
McRAY - See McCRAY
McRECTOR, McRICTOR, M. [1836-4]
McROBERTS, Andrew 184, [1836-6]
   Samuel 33, 80, 154, 184, 207, [1836-6]
McROY, A. [1836-8]
   Thomas [1836-8]
McSPADEN, McSPADDEN
   James [1836-16]
   Jno. M. 228
MACKIE, Benjamin 15
MADAUX, Nathaniel [1836-14]
MADDIN, MADDEN
   James 23, 94, 149, 195, [1836-10]
   Saml. 15, 23, 78, 135, 195
   William (Wm.) 23, 94, 149, 195, [1836-8]
MADOX, Joseph [1836-14]
MAGHEE, Jesse 8
   Wm. 8
MAINS, MANES
   Hiram 111, 124, 181, [1836-15]
MAISE - See MAYS
MAIZE - See MAYS
MAJOR, George W. [1836-7]
MALONE, Jno. 152
MANERY, MANRY, MANERLY
   Edward 59, 145, 212, [1836-13]
MANES - See MAINS
MANIS, Ephraim [1836-1]

MANKER, Bryon [1836-16]
MANNERS, Edward 32, 83
MANRY - See MANERY
MANSEL, MANSELL, MANZDE
   Burrel 23, 94
   Martha 149, 179, [1836-8]
   Robert (Robin) 23, 94, 149, 195, [1836-8]
MANVEL, Jno. G. 144
MANZDE - See MANSEL
MAPLES, Ephraim [1836-11]
   Jesse 156, 184
   Thos. [1836-11]
   William (Wm.) 18, 73, 147, 214, [1836-14]
MARKHAM, Josiah [1836-11]
MARLER, MARLOW
   George 23, 103, 149, 195, [1836-8]
MARSH, Alfred 115, [1836-2]
MARSHELL, MARSHAL, MARTIAL, MARCHAL
   John 195
   William (Wm.) 94, 149, 195, [1836-8]
MARR, George W. [1836-7]
MARTIN, MARTAIN, MARTON, MARTEN
   Charles W. 45, 106, 116
   E. W. 71
   Hugh E. 120
   Isaac 96, 124, 181
   John [1836-6]
   Joseph 8, 68, 164, 191
   Mathew 101
   Philip H. (may be Mastin) 225
   Robert 8, 68, 164, 211
   Samuel (Saml.) 30, 211, [1836-4], [1836-12]
   William [1836-12]
MARONY, Samuel [1836-12]
MARSTON - See MASTIN
MARTIAL - See MARSHELL
MASENGALE - See MASINGALE
MASHBURN, MASHBORN
   David [1836-15]
   John [1836-5]
   Mathew 197
MASON
   Tavner, (Tabner) 53, 60, 123, 199
   Wm. S. 45, 106
   Winson 199
MASONY, Samuel [1836-12]
MASSEY, Hugh 146
MASSINGALE, MASENGALE
   Adam (Adam G.) 18, 75, 159, 187, [1836-12]
   James 18, 75, 159, 187, [1836-12]
MASTIN, MASTON, MARSTON
   Holden 25, 89, 156
   John 75, 89, 159
   Jno. B. 133
   J. B. 35
   Philip H. (may be Martin) 225
   Reubin 18, 65, 75, 133, 159, 205, [1836-12]
   Thomas (Thomas W.) 18, 65, 75, 133, 159, 205, [1836-12]
MATLOCK
   Charles 4, 85, 139, 197, [1836-2], [1836-3], [1836-4], [1836-7]
   Henry 4, 85, 139, 197, [1836-4]
   John 23, 87, 118, 208, [1836-10]
MATTAX, Rachel [1836-15]
MATTHEWS, MATHEWS, MATHIS, MATHIES
   Allen H. 45, 106
   Aaron Estate [1836-4], [1836-7]
   Aron 45, 106, 116, 228
   Irvin (Erve) 27, 71, 121
   James [1836-5]
   John 25, 89, 156, 184, [1836-5]
   Lindsey 121
   Taltor, Paltor, Tarltor, 27, 71, 120
MAXFIELD, Benjamin [1836-10]
   David 50

James 50
Jno. 162
MAXWELL
   James 167, 220, [1836-15]
   John (Jno.) 167, [1836-15]
   Robert 25, 89, 156, 184, [1836-5]
   Wm. 25, 89, 156, 184
MAYFIELD, James 50
   Jesse 45, 106, 116, 228, [1836-17]
   Nancy [1836-17]
   Pearson B. 21, 63, 144
   Penelope [1836-7]
   P. Heirs of 202
   Thomas (Thomas B.) 45, 106, 116, 228, [1836-12]
   William 172, 227, [1836-7]
MAYO, Geo. W. 106, 115, 227
   James 115, 227
MAYS, MAZE, MAY, MAISE, MAIZE
   Caleb (Calip) 21, 62, 144, 202, [1836-17]
   James 4, [1836-1]
   John 21, 144, 202, [1836-17]
   John & Owen 63
   Owen 202
   Wm. 21, 62, 136, 144, 202
MEADLIN, Macklin [1836-16]
MEDARAS, Charles W. [1836-11]
MEDARIAS, William [1836-11]
MEDDERS, James 63
MEDERIS, John [1836-11]
MEIGS, Elizabeth 2, 167, 220, [1836-17]
   R.G. [1836-17]
   R. J. 45, 106, 116, 228
MELTON, Burrell [1836-10]
   Carter 78, 131, 179, [1836-10]
   Elijah 36, 65, 133
MENDENHALL, Isaac [1836-5]
   John [1836-2]
MENTON, MINTON, Johnson [1836-2]
MERONY, Philip 192
METCALF, MITCALF
   Charles 48, 101, 170, 189, [1836-3], [1836-4]

MEZELS, MEAZELS, MEASELS
   Luke 32, 83, 129, 225
MICHALES, MICHALZ
   Frederick 37, 96, 172, 181
MIERS - See MYERS
MIDDLETON, Charles 23
   Hugh [1836-6]
   John 25, 89, 156, 184, [1836-6]
MILLER, Adam 33, 80, 154
   Coonrad [1836-11]
   Elijah L. [1836-3]
   Jacob 200
   James 18, 75, 159, 187
   John 6, 47, 48, 58, 68, 80, 101, 136, 164, 169, 170, 191, 192, 204, 205, [1836-4], [1836-6] (2), [1836-7], [1836-11] [1836-15] (2)
   Leven [1836-4]
   Morgan [1836-6]
   Thomas (Thos.) 30, 87, 117, 118, 208 (2), [1836-10]
   Wm. 94
   William L. [1836-2]
MINTON - See MENTON
MINZE, Joseph 4, 85, 139, 197, [1836-4]
MIRES, Thomas [1836-16]
MISER, John 30, 78, 87, 118, 208
MISIER, Elijah [1836-10]
MITCALF - See METCALF
MITCHELL, MITCHEL
   Allen 8, 68, 164, 191, [1836-10]
   James 37, 96, 124, 181
   James C. (J. C.) 45, 106, 110
   Reace [1836-15]
   Thomas H. (Thos. H.) 211, [1836-15]
   William [1836-15]
   Zira 75
MONROE
   George 27, 71, 121, 178, [1836-2]
   Jesse 27, 71, 121, 178
   Robert 152, 200, [1836-2]
MONTGOMERY
   George 27, 71, 121, 178

MOODY, Andrew J. [1836-10]
  John [1836-1]
  Joseph C. [1836-10]
MOONEY, David 15, 78
MOORE, MORE, MOORS
  Alexander [1836-3]
  Caleb [1836-1]
  David 103, 172, 216, [1836-8]
  Jabus G. (Jabes G.) 50, 118, 208
  Jacob 109, 160, 161, 217, 218, [1836-17]
  James (James A.) 15, 78, 135, 179
  Jesse C. 33, 65, 154, 207, [1836-6]
  John [1836-4] (2)
  Kinsey 10, 103
  Little Berry (Little B.) 15, 78, 131, 211, [1836-11]
  Ransom J. [1836-13]
  Richard [1836-8]
  Samuel [1836-3]
  Stephen 111, 149, 195
  Thomas [1836-3]
  William (Wm.) 6, 58, 137, 192, [1836-4], [1836-15]
  William W. [1836-11]
MORELAND, MOORELAND, MORLAND
  George 4, 85, 139, 197
  John 2, 92
  Joseph [1836-15]
  Thos. 15
MORGAN
  George 45, 68, 106, 116, 164, 227
  Gideon (Gid) 37, 96, 228, [1836-16]
  John 12
  Joshua 8, 162, 218, [1836-15]
  Richard 37, 96, 127, 222, [1836-16]
  Samuel 218, [1836-15]
  Silas (Silas Sr.) 37, 96, 126, 222, [1836-16]
  Silas 111, 149, 195, [1836-16]
  Thomas 96
MORLAND - See MORELAND
MORRIS, Dickerson [1836-5]
  Dixon 2, 92, 152, 200
  Hardy S. 12, 60, 172, 199, [1836-9]
  James 109, 162, 218, [1836-17]
  Joe 116
  Jordin (Jorden) 23, 111
  John 18, 75, 136, 159, 192
  John Esq. [1836-12]
  Joseph B. 23, 111, 149, 195
  Little Berry 195
  Stephen 18, 75, [1836-12]
  Thomas 27, 71, 121, 178
  William (Wm.) 42, 109, 162, 170, 218, [1836-15]
  William M. [1836-15]
  William N. (W. N.) 195, [1836-3]
MORRISON, MORRISSON, MORISON
  [no first name] [1836-7]
  John (John B.) 48, 85, 139, 197
  Joseph B. [1836-4]
  Nathaniel (Nat.) 25, 89, 156, 184, [1836-4]
MORROW, James 21
MORTON, Silas [1836-10], [1836-15]
MOSS, David 6, 133, [1836-7]
  Edmund [1836-7]
  Edward 6, 58, 156, 184, [1836-15]
  Eli (Elie) 40, 55, 143, [1836-13]
  John 45, 106, 110, 116, 228, [1836-7]
  William (Wm.) 207, [1836-11]
MOULTON, Elijah 205
MOUNT, John 15, 78, 135, 179
MOUNTCASTLE
  George E. (George, G. E.) 45, 106, 115, 228
MOYERS, George 216
MULKEY, Harlen 164
  James H. 211

John Sr. 8, 68, 164
John A. 18
John N. 8, 68, 164, 173
Jonathan 8, 68, 164
William (Wm.) 21, 144, 202, [1836-17]
MULLINS, Daney 189
Richd. 101, 189
MUNCEY, Thomas W. 45
MURPHY, MURPHEY, MURPHREY
Edward 38, 172, 181
Heirs of James 12, 60, 127, 222
John 10, 23, 94, 103, 149, 195
John M. [1836-10]
Robert 12, 38, 60, 96, 111, 125, 127, 182, 222
William [1836-10]
MURRAH - See MURRY
MURRELL, MURRILL, G. M. 106, 115
Graham [1836-7]
O. G. 45, 106, 115, 227, Frontispiece, [1836-7]
MURRY, MURREY, MURRAH
John 65, 133, 205
Reny 38
MUSIC, John [1836-10]
MUSIE, John [1836-10]
MYERS, MIERS
Jordon (Georden) 50, 68

N

NAPIER
Archd. H. (A.H.) 8, 68, 164, 190, 191, [1836-10], [1836-11]
NEAL - See NEIL
NEELY, Joseph 48, 101
Wm. 48, 101, 170, 189
William H. [1836-2]
NEIL, NEAL, NEILL
Abraham B. (Abrm. B., A. B.) 164, 191, [1836-15]
Anderson [1836-4]
Bazel C. [1836-7]

John 3, 4, 65, 85, 137, 139, 197, 205, [1836-1], [1836-4], [1836-11]
John M. 8, 53, 68, 164, 173, 229
Peter A. [1836-7]
Prior 139
NELSON, Henry [1836-14]
James M. 23
John (John S.) 36, 214
NETHERLAND, James W. [1836-5]
NEWBORN, Wm. J. 228
NEWES, John 199
NEWLAND, James 48, 111, [1836-7]
NEWMAN
Alfred (Alfred C.) 10, 103, 141, 216, [1836-8]
Bird 27, 71, 121, 178, [1836-2]
Bird Jr. [1836-2]
Daniel (D.) 9, 10, 103, 140, 141, 215, 216
David [1836-8]
James [1836-12]
James G. (James J.) 129, 225
Jesse 112, 170, 189, [1836-2]
Jno. W. (John) 141, 216
John 184, [1836-8], [1836-11]
Joshua 170
Robert M. (Robert) 36, 65, 133, 205, [1836-12]
William (Wm.) 32, 103, 129, 141, 225, [1836-8], [1836-12]
NEWTON
Benjamin (Benj.) 12, 23, 94, 149, 195, [1836-9]
Edward 8, 68, 164, 191, [1836-15]
John 12, 30, 87, 118, 208
Thomas [1836-9]
NICHOLAS, Frederick [1836-16]
Walter K. [1836-11]
NIGHT - See KNIGHT
NORELL - See NORVEL
NORMAN

Bennet 43, 106, 116, 228, [1836-7]
William (Wm.) 23, 94, 149, 195, [1836-8]
NORRIS
   Archibald 21, 63, 145, 202
   John Jr. 18
   West [1836-12]
   Wright (Wyet) 18, 76, 159, 187
NORTH
   George 33, 80, 154, 207, [1836-6]
   Patton 33, 80
NORVEL, NORELL, Clinton 25
   Wm. 25, 89, 157, 184
NORWOOD, Thomas W. 45
NOX - See KNOX
NUTTER, Walter 228

O

O'DONALD, O'DONNALL, ODONALL
   Isaac 34, 80, 154, 207
   James 154, 207
   Maurese 45
   Thomas [1836-6]
O'KELLY, Nimrod [1836-16]
OBEY, Hiram 203
ODEN, Peter 23, 94, 149
   Vincent 195, 199
OFFICER, James 40, 146, 213
   Jefferson 34
   Samuel W (Saml. W.) 34, 154, 207, [1836-6]
OLDHAM, James T. 38
OLIVER, Isaac 121
ONLY, John 30, 87, 118
   Levi [1836-9]
ORMSLEY, Wm. 21
ORR
   James 2, 92, 152, 200, [1836-6]
   John V. 189
   John W. [1836-4]
   Joseph L. [1836-4]
   Mary [1836-4]

William (Wm.) 36, 48, 65, 101, 133, 205, [1836-12]
   Heirs of Wm. 170, 189
ORTON, James [1836-10]
OSWALT, Simeon 50, 99
OVERBY, Hiram [1836-10]
OWEN, OWENS
   Charles 27, 71, 121
   Daniel [1836-16]
   Enoch 8, 131, 211, [1836-8]
   Geo. 139, 197
   George P. [1836-1]
   John 216, [1836-3], [1836-12]
   Jonathan 141, 172
   P.C. [1836-16]
   Thomas [1836-12]
   Wilson 10, 65, 116, 228

P

P--ICE, Wily 83
PACE, Leonard W. 12
   Robert 4, 85, 139, 178
PACK
   George [1836-13]
   Jeremiah 83, 129, 225, [1836-6]
   Thomas [1836-13]
PAIN, PANE, PAYNE
   Lewis 8, 68, 164, 191, [1836-14]
PANGEL, PANGLE
   Andrew 32, 129, 225, [1836-6]
   James [1836-17]
PANE - See PAIN
PARKER, Aron 8, 68, 164, 191
   George [1836-11]
   John B. 191
   William 182
PARKISON
   James [1836-7]
   John 30, 87, 118, 209, [1836-10]
   Manuel C. (Manuel) 30, 87, 118, 208, [1836-10]
   Thomas [1836-10]

PARMER, Wm. 85
PARRIS, PARICE, PARRICE
   John W. (Jno., Jno. W.) 147,
      214, [1836-14]
   Lemuel [1836-14]
   Moses 21, 73, 143, 221, [1836-17]
   William (Wm.) 21, 73, 147, 214, [1836-14]
PARSON, PARSONS
   John 30, 87, 118, 208
   Thos. 30, 87, 118, 209
   William (Wm.) 30, [1836-10]
PATRICK, John 50, 162
PATT, John G. [1836-4]
PATTERSON, Harden 145, 203
   Robert (Robt.) 21, 63, 145, 203, [1836-5]
   Samuel (Saml.) 16, 78, 109, 131, 211, [1836-11]
   Silas M. 191, [1836-16]
   Trion [1836-15]
   William (Wm. T.) 8, 68, 164, 191, [1836-14]
PATTON - See also CHUNN
   Robert H. 21, 63, 145, 203
PATTY
   Benjamin (Benjn. W.) 34, 81, 154, 207, [1836-6]
   George O. 154, 207, 225, [1836-6]
   Jesse 27, 71
   Josiah 129, 225
   Odadiah (Obed.) 32, 83, 129, 225, [1836-6], [1836-12]
PAYNE - See PAIN
PEACE - See PIERCE
PEAK, PEAKE, Abel 152
   Bird 2, 92, 152
   Bluford [1836-10]
   Jacob 27, 72
   Shel. [1836-10]
PEARCE - See PIERCE
PEARSON - See PIERSON
PEELER, Abner 40
   Benjamin 40

PENN, Wm. 6, 58, 136, 193
PERCELL - See PURCELL
PERREN, John 94
   Judah B. (Judah B.F.) 216, [1836-8]
   Saml. 94, 141, 216
   Wm. 141, 216
PETERS, PETER
   Christian (Christen) 66, 133, [1836-7]
   Christopher 221
   Isaac [1836-5]
   Landon C. (Langdon, Landern C.) 36, 66, 172, 228, [1836-7]
PETTIT, PETTET, PETTETT
   Joel (Joll) 205, [1836-11]
   Francis [1836-10]
   Nehemiah-Heirs of 6, 58, 137
PHARRIS, PHARRISS - See FARRIS
PHILIPS, Abraham 40
   B. 172
   Baty 205
   Charles 34, 81, 154, 207, [1836-6]
   Eli 193
   Elkany [1836-6]
   Mason 40, 55, 143
   Oswell 216
   Robert 94, 149, [1836-9]
   Wm. 21, 34, 63, 81, 154
PICKENS
   Andrew 73, 147, 214
   Canady [1836-17]
   Charles A. [1836-15]
   Nancy 42, 73, 147, 214, [1836-5], [1836-15]
   Reece 42, 73, 145, 203
   Robert 6, 58, 137, 193, [1836-15]
PIERCE, PEARCE, PEACE
   Daniel 16, 131, 211, [1836-11]
   David 45, 106, 116, 228, [1836-7]
   Edmond 116
   Ephraim 48, 101, 112

Jacob 15, 78, 131
James 15, 78, 131, 211, [1836-11]
John 48, 101, 170, 189, [1836-8]
Lewis 211
Thomas 45, 106, 116
Western (Westonn) 45, 65, 106, 133, 205, [1836-11]
William 83
PIERSON
   Ally (Allay, Alla, Alley) 21, 63, 145, 203, [1836-17]
   Doctor 27, 85, 121, 178
   Edmond (Ed. W.) 78, 125, 228
   Jesse W. 145, [1836-17]
   Sherwood W. 27, 121, 178
   William L. (Wm. L.) 27, 72, 121, 178, [1836-2]
PIKE, James H. [1836-10]
   John B. [1836-10]
PITCHER, John 121, 178
PITMORE, Barn 8
PITNER
   Adam 38, 96, 125, [1836-16]
   John 23, 110, 173
PLANK, Benedict [1836-3]
   Christien [1836-3]
   Hiram [1836-3]
PLOWMAN, PLOUGHMAN
   Geo. 125, 211
   Jacob 38, 99, 164, 208
POE
   John 50, 99, 167, 220, [1836-17]
POLK, Charles 218
POLLY, Alexander 23
PONDER, John 48
   Nathaniel (Nat., Nanthrill) 48, 101, 170
POOLE, POOL
   Young A. 8, 68, 164, 191
POPE
   Fielding (F.) 45, 106, 116, 228
PORTER, Andrew [1836-6]
   Boyd [1836-7], [1836-8]

Henry H. (H. H.) 30, 87, 135, 223
James B. 23, 94, 149, 195
J. H. 77
John 200
John H. 15, 78, 131, 228
John R. 23, 94, 149, 195, [1836-8]
Robert (Robert S.) 30, 96, 125, 179, 182
William B. [1836-10], [1836-16]
Wm. C. (Wm.) 30, 96, 125, 182
Wm. 30, 78, 127, 131, 211
POTTER, James 218, [1836-17]
   Jesse [1836-17]
   Richard 12
   Solomon 48, 101, 170
   Wm. 38, 96, 223
POTTS, Amos 36, 65, 133, 205
POWELL, POWEL, Abraham 18
   George W. 205
   Scott [1836-8]
POWER, POWERS
   Holleway (Holloway, Holoway) 48, 101, 170, 189, [1836-3]
PRATHER, PRATER, PRATOR
   Danl. W. 131
   Edward 42, 109, 162
   John 16, 78
   Joseph 200
   Philip 8, 68, 164
   Saml. 36, 66, 133, 205
   Thomas 162, 182, 218, [1836-16]
   Wm. 16, 78, 131, 211
PREIST, John 27
PRESNELL, PRESNAL
   Elias 25, 89, 157, 184
   Ireal 152
PREWIT, Richard [1836-8]
PRICE
   Charles 23, 94, 149, 193, [1836-8]
   George W. (G.W.) 218, [1836-17]

Henry 23, 94, 149, 195
John W. [1836-8]
Washington 42, 109, 162
William (Wm.) 30, 87 (2), 125, 230, [1836-16]
Wm. W. 129
PRIGMORE
    Thomas 27, 71, 121, 178, [1836-1]
PRINCE, Andrew J. [1836-13]
    Isham [1836-11]
    Josiah [1836-13]
    Wiley [1836-13]
PRIVET, Francis J. 30
PROCTER, Benj. 78
    Hiram 178
PROFFIT
    Arrington, Arinton (Aronton) 6, 58, 137, 193, [1836-12]
PUGH
    Fleming C. 12, 61, 123, 199
    Hiram [1836-9]
    Hiram A. 12, 61
    John 12, 61, 123, 199, [1836-9]
    Jonathan [1836-9]
    Samuel [1836-5]
    Sarah [1836-9]
PURCELL, PURSELL, PERCELL
    Daniel 27, 71, 121, 178, [1836-2]
    Widow [1836-4]
PYRAM, James F. [1836-6]

Q

QUCK, John [1836-10]
QUEEN, John S. 179
QUEENER, QEENER
    Cyrus 123
    G.C. [1836-15]
    G.W. [1836-15]
    John 21, 145, 203, [1836-15]
QUITT, QUIOTT, QUEETT
    Cirus 110, 199
    Sirus [1836-9]

R

RABURN, Joseph 207
RAGAN, REAGAN, Daniel 101
    Ephraim 2, 92, 152
    James H. (Jas. H.) 2, 92, 150, 152, 200, [1836-5]
    Wm. S. 48, 101, 170
RAGLE, Wm. K. (Wm.) 38, 96
RAGSDALE
    Benjamin 16, 106, 116, 228, [1836-7]
    Jacob [1836-7]
    Wyley (Wiley, Willie) 27, 72, 121, 139, 197
RAINEY, John [1836-13]
RAINS, Philip 16
RAMEY, RAMAE
    Thos. 19, 76, 159, 187
RAMSEY
    Edmund 12, 110, 127, 223
    John 13, 127
    Lewis 110, 127, 223
    Nancy 110, 127, 223, [1836-9]
RANDOLPH
    Hezekiah 32, 83, 129
    Jeptha [1836-15]
    Lancaster (Lankester) 16, 79, 131, 211, [1836-15]
    Peyton (Paton, Payton Sr.) 8, 68, 165, 191, [1836-15]
    Pleasant 165, 191
    Robert (Robt.) 23, 94, 149, 195, [1836-8]
    William (Wm.) 8, 68, 165, 191, [1836-11]
RANEY, Jehue 218
RAY, WRAE, RHEA, REY
    Benjamin (Benj. F.) 48, 102
    Thomas 85, 139, 197
    Thos. I. 8, 68, 165, 191
    Wm. 8, 68, 165, 191
    Wm. W. 8
READING - See REDING

REAGAN - See RAGAN
REASILY, Hugh [1836-15]
REATHERFORD - See RUTHERFORD
REAVLY, Hugh [1836-15]
RECTOR, Jacob 30
    Maximillian 4, 85, 139, 197
REDFEREN, Hauzie [1836-8]
REDING, REDDING, READING
    Rebecca 27, 72, 121, 178,
        [1836-1]
    Thomas [1836-1]
REECE, Elijah [1836-10]
    Isaac [1836-10]
    John [1836-10]
REED, REID
    David (David Sr.) 16, 78, 131,
        228
    David Jr. 228
    George 25
    George W. (G.W.) 167, 220,
        [1836-16]
    James 45
    James T. [1836-7]
    Jeremiah 48, 101, 170, 189
    John 187
    J. T. 230
    Robert 16, 21, 63, 78, 131, 172
    Robert S. 228
    Samuel M. (Saml.) 63, 145,
        203, [1836-17]
    William P. (Wm. P., W. P.) 16,
        78, 109, 170, 228, [1836-7]
REEDER, Stephen 228
REESE, Elijah 87, 209
    Sherwood 30
REEVELY, REIVLY, RELEVER
    Francis 73, 147
    Hugh 214
REEVES, REAVES
    Ewell (Ewel) 40, 55, 143, 221
    Hugh 116
REID - See REED
REIVLY - See REEVELY
RELEVER - See REEVELY
RENEROW
    Robert 16, 78, 118, 223

RENNO, John 121
RENTFRO, Robert [1836-10]
RETHERFORD - See RUTHERFORD
REY - See RAY
REYNOLDS, REYNOLD, RUNNELS
    Daniel [1836-8]
    David 2, 92
    George 32, 83, 129, 225, [1836-
        6]
    Green L. 19, 73, 76, 147, 214,
        [1836-14]
    H. Estate [1836-12]
    Henry 19, 76, 159, 187, 228
    Humphrey 45, 106, 116, [1836-
        7]
    Isaac 187
    Isaac W. [1836-12]
    Isaiah [1836-12]
    Isham 19, 76, 159, 187
    Montreville [1836-7]
RHEY - See RAY
RHEYNHART - See RINEHART
RHINEHART - See RINEHART
RHOADS, ROAD
    David 32, 83, 129, 213, 225
RIAN - See RYAN
RICE, Charles W. [1836-10]
    Henry 184, [1836-5], [1836-17]
    Isaac 2, 92
    Jesse 16, 78 (2), 135, 180,
        [1836-8]
    John 16, 30, 78, 87, 118, 135,
        180, 209, [1836-8], [1836-
        13]
    Lani S. [1836-10]
    Lyman (Limon) 34, 81, 154,
        207, [1836-6]
    Martha 25, 89, 157, 184, [1836-
        5]
    Tandy 25, 45, 111, 157, 184
    William 123, 199
RICHARDS, RICHARD
    Adam 19, 76, 159, 187
    Asa 34, 81, 154, 207
    Daniel [1836-11]
    Fredk. (Fedrick) 101, 189

Nancy 81, 154, 207
Richard 36, 45, 106, 133, 229
Sam. [1836-12]
RICHARDSON, RICHESON, RICHERSON
   George 42, 109, 218
   James (Jas.) 152, 200, [1836-1], [1836-10]
   Jesse [1836-1]
   John 10, 103, 141, 216
   Jonathan 149, 195
   Martin 45
   Samuel [1836-10]
   Thomas 87 (2), 118, 209
   William (Wm.) 23, 94, 149, 195, [1836-8]
   Zadock [1836-9]
RICHEY, John [1836-6]
   William [1836-14]
RICHMOND, James 4, 85
RIDDLE, RIDLE
   Francis 48, 101, 170, 189
   James [1836-2]
   James J. 228
   John 30, [1836-2]
   Lewis 101, 170, 189
   Rolin 123
   Saml. 27, 72, 121, 178
   Samuel L. [1836-2]
RIDER, John [1836-4]
RIDLEY, William [1836-14]
RIGHT - See WRIGHT
RIGGINS, Lawson W. 10
   Thomas 48, 101, 135, 180, [1836-8]
   William (Wm.) 109, 135, 180, [1836-8]
   William P. (Wm. P.) 189, [1836-7]
RIGGS, RIGS, James J. [1836-13]
   Jesse, 213
   Samuel (Saml.) 40, 59, 146, 213, [1836-13]
   Wm. 59, 225
RINEHEART, RHINEHART, RHEYNHART
   Daniel 73, 159, 221
   Ephraim 76, 159, 221
   Joseph [1836-9]
   Lewis 53, 73, 159, 221, [1836-14]
RIPLEY, Jacob [1836-4]
   Miller & Co [1836-7]
   Thomas C. 101, 170
ROACH
   John Sr. (John) 13, 110, 123, 199
ROAD - See RHOADS
ROBBINS, Hance [1836-4]
ROBESON - See ROBISON
ROBERSON - See ROBISON
ROBERTSON - See ROBISON
ROBERTS, ROBERDS, ROBERD
   Benjamin 10, 103, 141, 216, [1836-3]
   Collins [1836-9]
   George [1836-10]
   Edmond 23, 94, 149, 195, [1836-8]
   Edmond W. 23, 94, 149, 195, [1836-8]
   George (F. N. -Free Negro) 180
   Hugh 72, 121
   James 2, 92, [1836-1]
   John 23, 50, 94, 99, 127, 149, 167, 195, 220
   Joseph 16, 79, 131, 211
   Joseph L. [1836-12]
   Joshua 36, 116, 228, [1836-12]
   Thomas M. (Thos. M.) 10, 103, 141, 195, [1836-8]
   William [1836-1]
ROBINETT, ROBINET, Allen 13
   Michael (Michel) 12, 110, 127, 223, [1836-9], [1836-10]
ROBISON, ROBESON, ROBERSON, ROBERTSON, ROBINSON
   Alexander C. (A. C.) 16 (2), 78, 131, 210, 211, [1836-11]
   Charles 38, 125, 182
   Daniel 32, 83, 129, 225, [1836-6]

Elizabeth [1836-4]
James 4, 85, 139, 197
John 4, 27, 72, 85, 121, 139, 197, [1836-5]
John H. 13, 61, 123
Joseph 45, 106, 116, 228, [1836-6], [1836-7]
Thomas 34, 81, 154, 207, [1836-6]
Wiley 225
William 197, 216
ROGERS
   Achilis (Achilles) 45, 106
   E.W. [1836 16]
   Henry [1836-16]
   James 23, 94
   James H. [1836-16]
   John 96, [1836-2]
   John Sr. [1836-16]
   Lawson 103, [1836-3]
   William (Wm. W., Wm.) 96, 125, 182, [1836-16]
ROLLINGS, George [1836-16]
ROMINES, Jasper 45, 106
ROPER, David 38, 96
   George (George W.) 123, 199, [1836-9]
   James 101, 170
   John M. [1836-9]
   Joseph 19, 76, 159, 187, [1836-14]
   Joseph L. [1836-12]
ROSE, Ephraim 180
   Saml. 6, 58, 137
ROSS, Lewis 172, 182, [1836-16]
   Nathaniel (Nathl.) 96, 125, 182, [1836-16]
ROTHNELL, ROTHWELL
   Richard 25, 89, 157, 216, [1836-3]
ROTIN, Vincen 203
ROWDEN, Abednego 10, 141
   Alkanah (Elkanah, Alkena) 10, 103, 141, 216
   Asa 103, 216, [1836-3]
   Elijah 10

James [1836-3]
John 10, 141, 216, [1836-3]
Meshac (Meshaka) 103, 141, 216
ROWELL, ROWEL, ROWLS
   [No name given] 173
   George [1836-16]
   Henry 154
ROYSTER
   Charles (Charles H.) 103, 216, [1836-3]
   Hardy (Hardy H.) 10, 103
   Harrison 141
RUBLE, RUBEL, Duke 195
   Peter 2, 92, 152
RUCKER, [No name given] 106
   James 16, 53, 79, 110, 135, 180, [1836-10]
   John 16
   Mordica (Modica) 19, 76, 159, 187, [1836-8]
   Wilford 16, 79, 135, 195
   Wm. 16, 79, 135, 195
RUDD, Herrod 45
   John 228
   Joseph 45, 106, 172, 228, [1836-7]
   Sarah (Mrs. Sarah) 106, 116, 228, [1836-7]
   Thomas 45, 106, 116, 228, [1836-7]
   William [1836-7]
   Wm. Sr. (Wm.) 45, 106, 116, 228
   Wm. Jr. 45, 106, 116, 228
   William H. 203
RUE, Joseph 129
RUNNELS - See REYNOLDS
RUSH, Absalom 4, 85
   Cyrus 139, 197
   John F. 228
   Noah 139
   Wm. 4, 85, 139, 197
RUSSELL, RUSSEL, Charles 25
   Curtis 89, 157
   James 19, 76, 159, 187

Joseph [1836-7]
Magor 21, 63, 203
RUSTEN, John [1836-5]
RUSTER, Hardy 23
RUTHERFORD, RETHERFORD, REATHERFORD
Edward 2, 92, 152
James 2, 92, 152, 200, [1836-1]
Larkin 159, 187, [1836-13]
Nehemiah (Nehimiah) 2, 92, 152, 200, [1836-4]
William [1836-1]
RYAN, RIAN
Albert G. [1836-17]
Amos 59, 146, 213, [1836-13]

S

S__AILOY, Jacob 160
SALLE, SALLEE, SALLEY, SALLIE
John [1836-4]
Joseph 48, 102, 170, 189
Masey [1836-2]
SALLER, John [1836-4]
SAMPLE, John 225
Samuel [1836-7]
SAMUEL, Charles P. [1836-7]
Easter [1836-11]
SANDERS, Clemmon 34, 154
Isaac 195
Richard 34, 129, 225
Wm. R. 42, 109, 162, 218
SANFORD, SANDFORD
Henry Sr. [1836-17]
Hezekiah (Hezekiah P.) 19, 76, 160, 187
SANTELL, Ephraim [1836-7]
SAPFORD, Henry Sr. [1836-17]
SARGENT, Albert [1836-11]
SARTON, Thos. 13
SATTERFIELD, Edward 21
James 74
SAUTELT, Ephraim [1836-7]
SAXON - See SEXTON
SAXTON - See SEXTON

SCARDROUGH, SCARBROW, SCARBOROUGH
James (Jas.) 16, 79, 131, 211, [1836-10]
John [1836-17]
Michael 99, 167, 220
Robert 50, 99, 167
William [1836-17]
SCELTON - See SHELTON
SCHELTON - See SHELTON
SCHOOL, John [1836-8]
SCODHAM, John 38
SCOTT, Robert 58, 137
James [1836-12]
Jesse [1836-2]
Manuel [1836-11]
SCRIMSHER, George 40
John 59
SEABOURN, SEABORN
James 13, 61, 110, 123, 199, [1836-9]
John 13, 61, 123, 199, [1836-9]
Joseph 13
McKinsey (Kinsey) 13, 61, 123, 199
SEAHORN, George [1836-7]
SEATON, William [1836-14]
SEAY, SEA
John (John L.) 8, 16, 69, 79, 131 (2), 165, 211
Obied 8
SELLERS
Edmond [1836-4]
Edward G. 16, 79, 135, 180
Fendley 121
James 28, 72, 121, 178
Mertle [1836-2]
Micah (Michael) 27, 72, 121, 178
Washington 189
William 121, 178
SENTER, CENTER, CENTERS
Francis K. (Fr. K., F.K.) 46, 100, 169, 188, [1836-4]
James 8, 69, 163, 165, [1836-15]

Martin 36, 66, 116, 183, [1836-10]
Schorn 46, 106, 110, 229
Stephen 38
Wm. (Wm. T.) 38, 96, 125
Willis S. 155, 183
SEWELL, SEWEL
   Dennis T. 40, 55, 143, 221
   George [1836-9]
   James [1836-9]
   James D. 58, 137, 193
   Jackson [1836-9]
   Sipy 170, 189
SEVILS, Absalam [1836-10]
   Wallace W. [1836-9]
SEXTON, SAXON, SAXTON
   Archibald 203
   Chisum 168
   James R. (James) 19, 50, 99, 172
   Russell 74
   Wm. 76
   William Jr. [1836-12]
SEYBERT, John [1836-15]
   John Jr. [1836-15]
SHADLE
   James 48, 102, 152, 201, [1836-4]
SHAFER, Merideth [1836-8]
   William [1836-8]
SHAMBLIN, SHAMBLEN
   Archibald 42, 109, 162, 218
   George [1836-15]
   John 42, 109, 162, 218, [1836-17]
   Wm. Sr. (Wm.) 42 (2), 109, 162, 218, [1836-15]
   Wm. Jr. 109, 162, 218
SHARP, SHARPE
   David [1836-2]
   Edward 13, 53, 61
   Eli 123, 199
   Hiram [1836-9]
   Jacob 13, 61, 123, 199, [1836-9]
   Joel 13, 61, 199, [1836-9]

Robert 13, 61, 123, 199, [1836-9]
SHEALS - See SHIELDS
SHEARLEY - See SHIRLEY
SHEARMAN, SHERMAN
   John 2, 92, 152, 201, [1836-5]
   Thomas 2, 92, 152, 201, [1836-5]
SHEFFLET, Austin [1836-8]
SHELL, Benjamin [1836-8]
   James [1836-4]
SHELTON, SCELTON, SKELTON, CHELTON, SCHELTON
   David 10, 103, 141, 216, [1836-8]
   James 13, 61, 123, 199, [1836-9]
   John 40, 59, 146, 213, [1836-13]
   Joseph 10, 103, 141, 216, [1836-8]
   Park 10, 103, 141, 216
   Saml. 103, 141, 216
   Stinson B. [1836-3]
   Thomas (Thos.) 21, 63, 145, 153, 162, 203, [1836-14]
   William (Wm.) 23, 94, 149, 195, [1836-8]
SHERRILL, SHERILL, SHIRELL, SHIRRELL
   Eli (Elie) 16, 79, 211, [1836-8]
   Isaac [1836-11]
SHERMAN - See SHEARMAN
SHIELDS, SHEALS, SHIELD
   Banner 21, 63, 145, 203, [1836-17]
   D & M & Co [1836-7]
   George A. (George H.) (160 a) 13, 110, 127, 223, [1836-9]
   George H. (George) (1 WP) 110, 127, 223
SHIPLEY, Aquiller [1836-16]
   Christopher 2, 92
   Elizabeth 152, 201, [1836-1]
   Equillia 50
   James [1836-1]

Randolph R. [1836-1]
Uriah 197
SHIRLEY, SHEARLEY
   John 13, 61
   Saml. 46, 154
SHIRRELL - See SHERRILL
SHOEMAKER, SHUMAKER
   Alfred 116
   John 86, 139, 197, [1836-1], [1836-2]
SHOOK, Isaac [1836-7]
   John 79, 180
   Wm. 46
   William Jr. [1836-7]
   William Sr. [1836-7]
SHOOPMAN
   Jacob 36, 46, 66, 106, 116, 205
   Wm. 30
SHORT, John B. [1836-15]
   Mary [1836-15]
SHOTE, Manuel [1836-11]
SHUGART, John C. [1836-10]
SHUMAKER - See SHOEMAKER
SHULTZE, SHULTS
   David 4, 85, 139, 197
SIBERT - See SYBERT
SIMONDS, SIMONS, SIMMONS
   John 32, 83, 129, 141
SIMPSON
   John 36, 66, 133, 205, [1836-12]
   Richard [1836-16]
SIMS, Vinson 116
   Wm. 11
SISCO, James 121
SISK, Alexander [1836-10]
SITZE, CITZE, SITZ
   Jesse 19, 75, 160, 187
   Lawson H. 160
   Margaret [1836-14]
SIVELS, SIVLES, SIVILLS
   Absalom 13, 127
   Wallace W. (Wallis W.) (W. W.) 13, 110, 127, 223
SLACK

Abraham L. (Abram. L.) 189, [1836-8]
A. D. 170
Saml. 189
SLAGER - See SLICER
SLAGLE, David 48, 102, 189
SLATON, James 116
SLAUGHLER, Isaac [1836-15]
SLAUGHTER
   John B. (John) 50, 220
   J. W. 50
   Wm. 50, 191
SLICER, SLAGER, SLYGER, SLIGAR
   Adam 27, 72, 121, 178, [1836-1]
   Henry [1836-2]
   Jacob 11, 103
   Thomas [1836-2]
SLOAN, SLONE, SLOANE
   Archibald 21, 63, 145
   James 21, 63, 145, 203
   Jno. 145
   Robert 21, 63, 145, 203
SLOVER
   Abraham 46, 106, 229, [1836-7]
SLYGER - See SLICER
SMALL, Harvey 2, 92
   Henry [1836-1]
   James (James A.) 2, 10, 92, 103, 141, 201, 216, [1836-4], [1836-5]
   John 4, 85, 139, 197, [1836-1]
   Mathew 11, 103, 141, 216
   William 2, 92, 152, 201, [1836-5]
   William W. [1836-5]
   Wilson 152, 201, [1836-5]
SMART, Thomas 199, [1836-9]
SMAYBAUGH, Jacob 187
SMEDLEY, SMEDLY, SMIDLEY
   Green 125
   John 38, [1836-16]
   John R. 38, 96, 125
   Thomas 38, 96, 125
   Wm. 38, 97, 125, 182
   Wm. Jr. 38, 97, 125, 182

Wm. Sr. 125
SMITH, SMYTH, SMITHE
   Abner 36
   Asa (Isa) 30, 87, 119, 211
   Berry 36
   Bowling (Boling) 46, 106
   Caleb 6, 58, 147, 193
   Collins [1836-15]
   David [1836-6]
   Edward [1836-3]
   Elisha 220
   Elitia [1836-16]
   D. Estate [1836-4]
   David 74, 147, 214
   Evan 58
   Gabriel C. 116
   George 50, 99, 168
   Gideon W. [1836-12]
   Gregory [1836-15]
   Henderson [1836-5]
   Henry 189
   Hugh 46
   Isaac 30, 87, 119, 209, [1836-10]
   Isaiah [1836-4]
   Israel (Izreal) 34, 81, 154, 207, [1836-6]
   Jackson 7, 8, 57, 58, 102, 137, 170, 192, 193, [1836-15]
   Jacob 36, 86
   James 4, 16, 19, 38, 53, 76, 79, 131, 211, [1836-10]
   Jesse 46
   Joel [1836-3]
   John, John S., John J., John W. 25, 76, 81, 123, 154, 160, 187, 189, 199, 207, 220, [1836-2], [1836-6] (2)
   Joseph 19, 25, 76, 81, 90, 97, 121, 152, 154, 160, 187, 201, 207, 220, [1836-1], [1836-5], [1836-6]
   Levi 223
   Loftam N. [1836-15]
   Lowry [1836-11]
   Loyd 16
   Margaret 19, 76, 160, 187
   Mary 25, 81, 154, 207, [1836-6]
   Nathaniel (Nat.) 46, 48, 102, 116, 152, 170, 189, 201, [1836-4], [1836-7]
   Nathl. F. 116
   Riley 11, 103
   Robert 19, 76, 160, 187, [1836-6], [1836-12], [1836-14]
   Russel [1836-11], [1836-12]
   Saml. 68, 145
   Sarah 50
   Silas 193, [1836-15]
   Sharkman D. [1836-5]
   Stephen 170, [1836-4]
   Theophilas [1836-2]
   Thomas (Thomas M.) 25, 90, 157, 184
   William (Wm.) 25, 30, 87, 146, 213, [1836-6] (2)
   Wm. Jr. 4
   William Sr. [1836-6]
   Wm. D. 119, 209
   William W. [1836-11]
   Williamson 116, ???
   Willis 127, 223
SNIDER, Robert [1836-3]
SNODDY, Saml. [1836-15]
SOATHARDS - See SUTHERD
SOLOMON, Daniel 199
SOWERBEER, John 229
SPARKS, SPARK
   Abijah [1836-16]
   William 83, 129, 225, [1836-12]
SPEARMAN
   Thomas (Thos.) 23, 94, 135, 180, [1836-8]
   Wesley 23, 94, 135, 180, [1836-10]
SPENCER, James [1836-2]
   Jesse B. 116
   John 27, 72
   Levy [1836-2]
   Levi, Jr. (Levi) 72, 121, 178
   Levi, Sr. 27, 72, 121, 178

SPRADLING, SPRADLIN
   [No name given] 11
   Overton 216
   Richard 103, 141, 216
   Richard Jr. [1836-3]
   Richard Sr. [1836-3]
   Standley 48, 141
SPRIGGS
   Ezekiel 40, 55, 142, 143, 221
ST. JOHN, Nathan [1836-6]
STAFFORD
   Joseph [1836-11]
   Nathan [1836-11]
   Thomas 154, 207, 225
   Wm. 96, 125, 182
STAGS, STAGGS, Saml. 79
   Thos. 79, 135
   Walter 79, 135
   Wm. 135, 180
STAINER - See STANNER
STALCUP, STALKUP
   Isaac 25, 90
   Moses 25, 90, 157, 184, [1836-5]
STAMBURY - See STANSBURY
STANDSBURY - See STANSBURY
   Israel (Isreal) [1836-1]
   Samuel [1836-1]
STANFIELD
   James 221, [1836-16]
   John [1836-9]
   Vinson W. 50
STANNER, STAINER
   Coonrod 23, 94, 149, 195, [1836-9]
STANSBURY, STANDBURY, STANBURY, STANBERY, STAMBURY
   Israel (Isreal) [1836-1]
   Samuel (Saml.) 32, 83, 152, 201, [1836-1]
   Thomas (Thos.) 40, 59, 146, 213, [1836-13]
STARLING - See STERLING
STARR
   Caleb 40, 55, 143, 221, [1836-13]
   James 199
STEED, STEAD
   Henry 25, 90, 116, 157, 184, 229, [1836-5], [1836-7]
   James (J.) 46, 106, 116, 229
   James Jr. [1836-7]
   James Sr. [1836-7]
   John (and No name given) 46, 106, 116, 229, [1836-7]
   Thomas (Thos.) 25, 90, 157, 184, [1836-5]
STEPHENS, David 6, 125
   James 6
   Nehemiah 125
   Philip 152
STEPHENSON, STEPHESON, STEPHISON, STEVENSON, STEPENSON
   Alex. 32, 83, 129, 225
   Andrew 6, 58, 137, 193, [1836-15]
   Edward [1836-6]
   James M. 209
   John 129, 225, [1836-12]
   Robert 36, 66, 133, 205, [1836-12]
   Standhope 119
   William Sr. (Wm. S., W.S.) 209, [1836-15], [1836-16]
   William W. [1836-16]
STEPP, David 123, 199
   Lucy 199, [1836-9]
   Wm. Jr. (Wm.) 13, 61, 123
   Wm. Sr. 199
STERLING, STARLING
   John B. (John) 11, 103
STEWART, STUARD, STEWARD, STUART, STEWERT
   David [1836-8], [1836-10]
   David Jr. 23, 94, 150, 195
   David Sr. 23, 94, 150, 195
   Hamilton (Hambleton) 23, 94, 150, 195, [1836-9]
   James [1836-9]

James P. 53
John D. [1836-10]
Saml. P. 61, 123
William (Wm.) 216, [1836-3]
STIFF, Wm. H. 182
STILLWELL, Jeremiah [1836-13]
STOCKTON, STOCKDEN
   Daniel D. 53, 103, 141, 216, [1836-3]
STOKER, Hillary (Hilery) 19, 76
STOKES, STOAKS
   Edward S. [1836-8]
   Henry R. [1836-9]
   Sylvanius (Silvinas, Sylvanis) 23, 94, 149, 195, [1836-9]
STONE, Ambrose [1836-1]
   Daniel 102
   Edward [1836-15]
   John 4, 85, 139, 197, [1836-1]
   Thos., -Black man-F. N. 23, 94, 180
STOUT, Benj. C. 46
   Benjamin Estate (Heirs of B.C.) 106, [1836-7]
   Daniel 170, 189, [1836-8]
   Jane 116
   Moses 46
STOW, Robert [1836-5]
   Samuel [1836-5]
   Solomon [1836-5]
STRANGE
   Fletcher [1836-11]
   Jeremiah F. 16, 79, 109, 131, 211
STREET, John [1836-16]
STUARD - See STEWART
STUART - See STEWART
STUBLEFIELD, STUBBLSFIELD
   Mahala [1836-12]
   Robert (Robt.) 187, [1836-12]
   Wm. 19, 76, 160, 187
STUDDARD, STUDARD
   Thomas 36, 66, 133, 205, [1836-12]
SUDATH, SUDITH
   James (J.) 8, 203

Luis 203
SULLINS, Jno. S. 127
   Nathan 16, 79, 116, 229, [1836-7], [1836-8]
SUMMERS, Hamilton [1836-16]
SUTHERD, SUTHARD, SOATHARDS
   Gillian (Gillum) 25, 90, 157, 184, [1836-4]
   Reuben P. [1836-12]
SUTHERN, SUTHERAN
   Nathan 220
   Noler 168
SUTTERFIELD, James [1836-14]
SUTTLES, Celia 170
SWAFFORD, Alfred [1836-15]
   Richard [1836-15]
   Thos. [1836-15]
SWAN
   James B. 34, 81, 154, 207
   John 34, 81, 154, 184, [1836-6]
   Robert M. 33, 34, 81, 154, 207, [1836-6]
SWINFORD
   Jonathan 165, [1836-16]
SWOPE, James 46
SYBERT, SIBERT, SEYBERT
   John S. 69, 165, 191

T

TAFF, George 2
   Peter 2
TALLENT, TALENT, TALLANT
   Enoch (Eanic) 109, 135, 180
   James [1836-8]
   Malacia (Malica, Maliki) 30, 119, [1836-10]
   Richard 16, 79, 135, 180
   William [1836-9]
TALLY
   Willis [1836-3]
TANKERSLEY, TANKSLEY, TANKERLY
   Andrew 160, 187
   Richard 34, 36, 109

Wm. (Wm. W.) 36, 66, 162
TANNER
   Thomas 42
TATE
   James 121, 173
   John 90
TAWBOT - See TORBUT
TAYLOR, TAILOR
   Baldwin H. (B.H.) 40, [1836-12]
   Charles (Charley) 38 (2), 61, 97, 127, 223
   George (George W., G. W.) 21, 63, 147, 214
   Henderson 143
   James 137
   John (Jno. W.) 72, 121, 172, [1836-1]
   Larkin 11, 104, 141, 216, [1836-10]
   Levi [1836-16]
   Newton 203
   Samuel [1836-17]
   Washington 225
   Wm. L. 21, 62, 63
TEAGUE
   J. P. M. C. 195
   Joseph 13, 61
TEAL
   William [1836-16]
TEAFATALLER - See TEFFETALLER
TEDFORD
   James 97, 125, 182
   John 50, 99
   Ralph E. [1836-17]
TEFFETALLER, TEFETALUR, TEAFATALLER
   Joseph 25, 90, 157
TELLISON - See TILLISSON
TEMPLETON
   James A. 30
   John (John H.) 30, 87, 119
   Nancy 87, 119, 209
TERRY
   William 2, 92, 157, 184, [1836-5]

THIM?, Anderson [1836-1]
THOMAS, THOS.
   Andrew 28
   George 36, 66, 134, 205
   James 4, 86, 139, 197, [1836-1], [1836-5]
   James Jr. [1836-1]
   John 25, 90, 157, 185, [1836-13]
   Jonathan 11, 104, 141, 216, [1836-1], [1836-3], [1836-5]
   Joseph 25, 90, 157
   Juliet [1836-11]
   Nathan 25, 90, 157, 185
   Saml. 102, 135
   Wm. Sr. (Wm.) 25, 90, 157, 185
   Wm. Jr. 157, 185, [1836-5]
   Williamson [1836-5]
THOMPSON
   A.B. [1836-7]
   Alexander 16, 79, 131, 211
   Alfred 40, 59, 146
   Daniel 40, 160, 187, 213, [1836-12]
   George W. (G. W.) 46, 107, 116, 229
   James 28
   James B. (James R., James) 8, 69, 165, 211
   John 6, 36, 53, 58, 76, 129, 137, 193, 225, [1836-11], [1836-12], [1836-15]
   John A. 16, 79, 131, 211, [1836-11]
   John C. [1836-8]
   John Jr. [1836-11]
   Lemuel Est. [1836-12]
   McRanda (Meranda, Machranda) 59, 146, 213
   Robert (Robt.) 40, 59, 146, 213, [1836-13]
   Mary (Admnt.), Saml's Admns., Saml. Heirs 40, 59, 146, 213

Saml. 40, 59, 146, 213
Samuel W. 119, 209, [1836-11]
Thomas (Thos.) 8, 69, 165, 191, [1836-15]
Wm. and Wm. Sr. 6, 23, 30, 69, 87, 94, 119, 150, 165, 191, 195, 209
Wm. D. 58
Williamson [1836-11]
THORNBURY, THORNBERY
  Louvina (Louvena, Lovina) 168, 220, [1836-16]
  Martin 11
  William [1836-16]
THORNHILL
  Barnet (Barnebas) 38, 97
  Robert 124
THORNTON
  Charles T. 207, [1836-6]
THORP, THORPE
  Harris D. (H. D.) 46, 107, 116, [1836-7]
TILLISSON, TELLISON
  Spencer 40, 55, 134, 205
TIMSLIN ?, William 99
TINKER, Jno. 139, 197
TINNEY
  Isaac 74, 147, 214, [1836-14]
  William [1836-14]
TITSWORTH
  Jesse 25, 90
TIPTON
  Esau [1836-4]
TODD
  Wm. 86
TOLBERT - See TORBUT
TOMLIN, [No name given] 97
TOMPSON - See THOMPSON
TORBUT, TORBETT, TOLBERT, TAWBOT
  John 32, 83, 225, [1836-6]
TOUCHSTONE
  Solomon 6
TOWNSEND, TOWERSON
  Thomas 8, 69, 165
TRAMMEL, TRAMMAL, TRAMELL
  James 30, 79, 87, 135
TREADWAY, TREADAWAY
  [no name] 34, 81, 154, 207
TRIBBLE
  Stephen [1836-8]
TRIPLET, TRIPLETT
  Joel 36, 66, 134, 205, [1836-7]
  Lewis 19, 76, 160, 193, [1836-12]
  Nimrod 36, 66, 134, 211, [1836-11]
  Wm. 36, 66, 134, 205
TRIPLIN
  Francis [1836-9]
TROTTER
  George 193, [1836-11]
  Isham 6, 58, 137, 193
  James 46, 107, 117, 229
  Patrick 107, 117
  P.T. [1836-7]
TROUBLEFIELD
  Abel 55, 214
  Iradle, Jradle 143
TROUT
  John 25, 90, 157, 185, [1836-5]
  Mathew [1836-5]
  Michael 25
  William (Wm.) 90, 157, 185, [1836-5]
TRUE, Thomas [1836-17]
TRUSTEES OF ATHENS ACCD. 46, 107
TRUSTEES OF FOREST HILL ACCD. 46, 107
TUCK, Joseph [1836-6]
  William [1836-6]
TUCKER, Gardner 213
  James S. 229
  John 46, 61, 107, 123, 170, 199
  Robert 117, 172
  Saml. 50
  Thomas [1836-8]
  Wm. R. 46, 107, 116
TUNNELL
  John 6, 58, 137, 193
TURK

Archibald R. (Archd. R., A. R.) 46, 107, 112, 117, 199, 229, [1836-16]
TURLEY, TURNLEY
Charles 61, 123
James A. (James) 38, 97, 127, 223
Mathew J. 25
TURNER
Daniel 28, 72, 121, 178
TURNLEY
[No name] [1836-16]

U

UNDERDOWN, George [1836-17]
UNDERWOOD
Alexander 13, 61, 124
John 199
Wm. 61, 124
UPSHAW, Drury 11
Forest 83
URRY, Jacob 107
UTLEY, E. H. 50

V

VANCE, Robert 135, 180, [1836-8]
Wm. 13, 61, 124, 199
VANDERFORD, Nathan 229
VANDYKE, T. Nixon [1836-7]
VARNELL, James 38, 97, 125
John 38, 97, 125, 182
Wm. 38, 97, 125, 182
VARNOLD, David N. [1836-16]
Elizabeth [1836-16]
VASSER, Daniel 13
VAUGHN
Mumford [1836-17]
Thomas (Thos.) 19, 76, 137, 160, 193, [1836-14], [1836-15]
VESTALL, VESTELL, VESTTLE
James 28, 72, 121, 178, [1836-1]
VETTNGGER, Joseph 220
VICKERS, VICKARS, Elijah 16
Thomas 16, 79, 135, 180
VICON, Thomas [1836-8]
VINCENT, VINZANDT, VANZANDT, VINSANT, VINZANT, VINSON, VANZANT
Charles 16
Elisha 9
Ezekial 9, 69, 165, 191
Jacob 13, 110, 127, 223
John (John Sr.) 9, 69, 165, 191
John Jr. 191
Jonathan 30, 220
Josiah 203
Nancy [1836-15]
Reubin (Reuben) 9, 69, 173, 191, [1836-16]

W

WADKINS, WATKINS
Mary [1836-15]
William (Wm.) 40, 60, 146, 213, [1836-12], [1836-13]
WADE, WAID
Elijah [1836-17]
James 104, 141, 216, [1836-3]
WAGGONNER, WAGNER
Jesse 4
M. M. 46
WAID - See WADE
WAKEFIELD
Alexander 36, 66, 134, 206, [1836-12]
Charles (Charls) 36, 66, 134, 206, [1836-12]
Thomas 36, 66, 134, 206, [1836-7]
WALKER, Caswell 107
Charles 145
C. M. D. 229
Edmund [1836-9]

Elias 34, 81, 154, 207, [1836-6]
Emily S. [1836-7]
Geo. W. 141, 216
Henry 16, 79, 131, 211, [1836-11], [1836-16]
Holton (Holtin) 11, 104, 141, 216
James 42, 109, 162, 218, [1836-9], [1836-17]
James E. [1836-9]
Capt. James 61, 127 (this is probably the James of Robert)
James (of Robert) (James) 13, 61, 127, 223
John [1836-9]
John Jr. 79, 117
John Sr. (John) 13, 61, 127, 223
Robert 13, 61, 223, [1836-9]
Washington 104
William (Wm.) 21, 74, 104, 147, 214, [1836-9] (page 104 is probably another Wm.), [1836-17]
William A. (Wm.) 145, 203
Wm. D. 23, 111, 150, 195
Wm. H. 23, 111, 150, 195
WALLACE, Israel 154
George [1836-1]
WALLING, WALDING, WALING, WALLEN, WALLON, WALLIN
Elizabeth [1836-15]
Isaac 220, [1836-15]
James 50, 100, 168, 220, [1836-11], [1836-17]
Jesse 50, 100, 125, 220, [1836-16], [1836-17]
Jno. 139
John [1836-1], [1836-16]
Thomas 4, 50, 86, 139, 168, 197, 220, [1836-1], [1836-15]
WALTENBARGER
Michael [1836-3]
Peter [1836-3]
WAMBLE

Wm. 40, 59, 146, 213
WAN, Robert [1836-2]
WARD
Benjamin (Benjn.) 23, 94, 150, 195, [1836-8]
Ezekiel [1836-10]
WARE - See WEAR
WARREN, Andrew 143
WASHAM, WASSOM, WASSAM, WASSON, WARSHAM
Benjamin (Benj.) 30, 87, 209, [1836-10]
Coonrod 28, 72, 122, [1836-2]
David 2
David C. (D. C.) 36, 66, 134, 206, [1836-7]
Elihu 117, 206
Harwood 178
James 4, 139
Jonas 86, 197, [1836-1]
Jonathan 2
Lonas [1836-4]
M. N. L., Maxamillians, M. 36, 107, 173
William (Wm.) 36, 66, 134, 206, [1836-7]
WATERHOUSE, Richard [1836-16]
WATERS, Lewis 19
Isaac [1836-10]
Moses [1836-10]
Peter J. 41
WATKINS - See WADKINS
WATSON, George [1836-6]
James [1836-6]
John [1836-6]
William (Wm.) 154, 207, [1836-6]
WAUMUCK, John [1836-3]
WEAR, WERE, WEIR, WARE
Abraham B. 21, 74, 147
Allen 9, 69, 165, 191
Berry 218
David 223, [1836-16]
George 25, 46, 90, 157, 229, [1836-5]

John 21, 63, 145, 203, 223,
   [1836-16], [1836-17]
Jno. H. 127
John M.C. [1836-16]
Samuel (Saml.) 21, 63, 145,
   203, [1836-17]
WEATHEN, Joseph [1836-4]
WEATHERLY, WEATHERALLY,
   WEATHELY, WHEETHLY,
   WEATHERDLY
   Hiram 19
   Jobe [1836-14]
   Mary 41, 111, 143, 221, [1836-14]
   Moses 10
   Saml. 143, 214
WEATHERS, George 30, 87
   Joseph [1836-4]
WEAVER
   Adam (Addam) 4, 86, 139, 197, [1836-1]
   John 21, 63, 145, 203
   Wm. 21, 63, 145, 203
WEBB, Allen 28, 72
   Calberth 178
   Gideon 13
   John 61
   Joseph [1836-4]
   Julius 13, 61
   Martin [1836-4]
   William 28, 72, 122
WEEKS, WEAKS
   David 50, 100
   Hiram 50, 100
   Solomon 38
   Wm. 50, 100
WEISE, Allen [1836-11]
   Tom [1836-7]
WEIR - See WEAR
WELKER, WELCKER
   Mrs. 117
   Wm. L. 46, 107
   Admns. of Wm. L. 229
WELLS, Jesse 19, 76, 160, 187
   Rusel 187
   Stephen 193, [1836-11]

Thomas P. (Thos.) 21, 63, 145,
   203, [1836-14]
WERE - See WEAR
WERI, George [1836-5]
WEST, Enoch [1836-2]
   Jesse [1836-2]
   Thos. 21
   William (Wm.) 46, 117, [1836-4]
WESTMORELAND
   Alexander 119
   Edward 209
   George 119, 209
WESTWOOD, WESTWARD
   John 6, 58, 66, 134, 206, [1836-16]
WHEAT - See WIATT
WHEELER, WHEELOR, WHELER
   Gabriel (Gabrel) 42, 147, [1836-14]
   James 11, 104, 142, 216, [1836-3]
   Samuel (Saml.) 11, 104, 141, 216, [1836-3]
WHEET - See WHIAT
WHEETHLY - See WEATHERLY
WHETSON ?, John 199
WHIAT - See WIATT
WHITE, A. D. 170, 229
   Barton [1836-2]
   Commadore [1836-12]
   Daniel 41, 60, 146, 213, [1836-13]
   Elisha 41, 60, 146, 213, [1836-13]
   Elizabeth [1836-12]
   Howell 58, 137, 193
   James 117, 229, [1836-7]
   James G. (James) 69, 165, 191
   Jesse 41, 59, 146, 213, [1836-13]
   John 21, 63, 145, 203, [1836-12], [1836-16], [1836-17]
   John (another one) 134, 206
   John D. (John B.) 66, 127
   Jonathan 19, 76, 160, 187

Moore John [1836-15]
Nathanl. (Ewing's Co.) 36, 134, 206
Nathanl. (Firestone's Co.) 19, 76, 160
Obediah (Obabiah) 23, 94, 150, 216, [1836-8]
William (Wm.) 50, 109, [1836-15]
Wm. (another one) 9, 69, 165, 191
Wm. H. [1836-12]
Wm. R. 13
WHITECOTTON, Bury [1836-16]
WHITEHEAD, Frances [1836-1]
WHITLEY, Martin 2
WHITMORE, WHITEMORE
John 9, 168, 220
WHITSELL, WHETSELL
Angeline 229
Michael 107, 117
WHITTEN, WHITTIN, WHITTON, WITTEN
Archibald 42, 109, 162, 218, [1836-16]
James 72, 122, 178, [1836-2]
John W. 178
Jonathan 218, [1836-16]
Stephen 81
Thos. V. 28
Wiley 122
William (Wm.) 162, [1836-17]
WHITTLE, Wm. [1836-11]
WIATT, WHIAT, Alfred [1836-15]
Drury (Drewry) 42, 109, 162, 218, [1836-15], [1836-17]
James 117
WIGGINS, WIGGINGS
John [1836-6]
William (Wm.) 32, 83, 129, 225, [1836-6]
WILHITE, Caleb 199
Kinsey 168
WILKERSON, Lawson [1836-17]
WILKINS
Rubin (Reubin) 206, [1836-7]

WILLEN, James [1836-2]
WILLIAMS, WILLIAM
Alexd. 131, 211
Andrew 13
Casander ?, 220
Daniel 9, 109, [1836-16]
Frederick 50, 109, 165
Frederick S. 25, 81, 154, 207
James G. 38, 97, 125, 182
Jesse 109
John 9, 69, 165, 191, [1836-8], [1836-11], [1836-12]
Mathias 28, 72
Peter 109, 168
Robert 117
Sarah [1836-11]
Shederick 50, 109, 220
Thomas L. 46, 107
William [1836-10]
WILLIS, WILES, WILIS
Marshal (Marshal S.) 107, 211
Saml. 36, 94, 150, 195
Wm. 34, 94, 150
Wright 180
WILLITT, Thomas 173
WILSON
Andrew M. (A. M.) 36, 66, [1836-14]
Absolem (Absalem)131, 229, [1836-11]
Alexander H. (Alexander) 25, 90, 157, 185
Benjamin [1836-17]
Benjamin W. 218
Cates 209
David 25, 90, 157, 185, [1836-5]
Elijah 191
Enoch 38, [1836-15]
George 50, 97, 125, 182
Hugh P. (H. P.) 25, 90, 157, 185, [1836-11]
James 66, 134, 206, 218, [1836-4], [1836-11], [1836-16], [1836-17]
James W. 42, 109, 162, 218

John 142, 193, 216, [1836-3]
John S. 9, 11, 69, 172
Joseph 187, [1836-4]
J. S. 67
Ransom 23
Richard 9, 69, 165, 191, [1836-15]
Samuel (Saml.) 34, 81, 119, 154, 207, [1836-5], [1836-6]
William (Wm.) 69, 134, 162, 165, 191, 193, 206, [1836-4], [1836-15]
William B. (Wm J.B., Wm. J. D.) 109, 162, 218, [1836-17]
Wm. H. [1836-12]
Wm. R. 30, 87, 119, 209
WINKLE
　Abraham 4, 86, 139, 173, 197, [1836-1]
WINTERS
　Christopher 46, 107, 117
WINTON
　George 90, 157, 185, [1836-5]
WIRICH - See WYRICK
WISEMAN, Martin 199
　Thomas D. 2, 92, 152, 201
WITT, WITTE, Abner 46, 107
　Burgess 56, 59, 143, 221, [1836-13]
　Ephraim (Ephraim H.) 36, 66, 172, 206, [1836-11]
　Harvey 143
　Hezekiah 40, 56, 143, [1836-13]
　James 48, 97, 110, 170, 173, 189, [1836-4], [1836-8]
　James H. [1836-14]
　Joseph 16, 79, 135, 180, [1836-8]
　Joshua 41, 56, 143, 221
　Mary 109, 135, 180, [1836-8]
　Morning 79, 135, 180
　Rutherford (Acatherford) 56, 143, 221, [1836-14]
　Silas [1836-8]
　Silas Jr. (Silas) 16, 135, 180
　Silas Sr. (Silas) 16, 79, 135, 180
　Valentine 41, 59, 146, 213, [1836-13]
　William (Wm.) 56, 143, [1836-13]
WITTEN - See WHITTEN
WITTENBURG
　Christopher 2, 92
　John 2, 92
　Wm. 2, 92
WOLF, A. B. C. 41, 56
　Daniel [1836-10]
　Elizabeth 182, [1836-16]
　George W. 41, 56
　Jeremiah 102, 142, 189
　John 97, 111, 125, [1836-15], [1836-16]
　Mary E. 125, 182
　Samuel [1836-15]
WOMAC, Daniel [1836-8]
　Jacob [1836-8]
WOMBLE, William [1836-13]
WOMLITE, William [1836-13]
WOOD - See WOODS
WOODALL
　Avarilla 50, 100, 168, 220
　David 50, 100, 168, 220
　Isaah (Isah, Isaiah) 168, 220, [1836-16]
　John 50, 100
WOODARD, WOODWARD
　Alexd. 229, [1836-7]
WOODFOLK, Hiram J. 117
WOODS, WOOD
　James 13, 61, 124, 165, 199, [1836-9]
　Joseph B. 162
　Peter 58
　Stephen 46, 107, 117, 229
　Thomas G. 229
　Vinson (Vincen, Vincent) 50, 100, 168, 220, [1836-11]
　Wm. 19, 76, 129, 160, 173

WOODWARD - See WOODARD
WOOTEN, John S. [1836-9]
WORKMAN
    Samuel (Saml., S.) 38, 97, 111 (2), 124, 125, 126, 181, 182, 222, [1836-7]
WORLEY, WORLY
    Hiram 107, 117, 229, [1836-7]
    Joseph 46, 107, 117
WRAE - See RAY
WRIGHT, WRYHT, RIGHT
    Benjamin 16, 79, 131, 191, [1836-11]
    Mary 173
    Robert [1836-4]
    Sydney [1836-5]
    William [1836-2]
    Willis [1836-8]
WYRICK, WIRICH
    Frederick 28, 72, 122, 178

Y

YANCY, YANCEY, YANCE
    Alexander 6, 58, 137, 193, [1836-14]
    Cyrus 21, 63, 145, 203
    Hiram 182
    Maridy [1836-14]
YATEE
    Saml. 60, 129, 213, 225
YOUNG
    Girshum 129
    Isaac 30, 87, 119
    Jacob 117
    John 30, 87, 119, 195, [1836-8]
    John F. [1836-10]
    Moses [1836-12]
    Nathan M. 102
YOUNT
    Peter 117, 229
YOURG, Mrs. [1836-7]
YOURY, Mrs. [1836-7]

Z

ZEGLER, ZEGLAR, ZEAGLER, ZEIGLER
    Michael [1836-8]
    Rachel 150, 195, [1836-8]
    William (Wm.) 23, 94, 150, 195 [1836-9]
ZENORE - See McPHERSON

www.ingramcontent.com/pod-product-compliance
Lightning Source LLC
Chambersburg PA
CBHW070455090426
42735CB00012B/2565